POEMS FOR IDLE MOMENTS

by
Godfrey Sparks

For Val
Forever

Date of Publication:
1ˢᵗ August 2014

© Copyright 2014 Godfrey Sparks

Printed by:
The City Press
Chatham
Kent
ME4 4RE

ISBN: 978-0-9927656-3-7

Further copies may be obtained from the Publisher, Godfreysparks@aol.com, or from the usual retail outlets quoting the ISBN ref. Price £6.00 plus p&p.
All proceeds are pledged to
The Pilgrims Hospice Ashford Kent.

The Painting on the front cover is a section from an acrylic by Paul C. Milner reproduced with his kind Permission.

Introduction

Congratulations Dear Reader to have got this far. Quite a decision picking up a book of modern verse – even if it was probably in a charity shop. I hope it gives as much pleasure to you reading it as it did to me in the writing. I should warn you – you won't find any "Golden Daffodils" or "Beaded Bubbles winking at the brim" though there is a bit of "Rage, rage against the dying of the light". Mostly its light verse about people – the living, the nearly dead and the definitely dead.

The old legal test used to be the man on the Clapham Omnibus – could he reasonably hold these views? It will shortly be for you to decide.

As a provincial solicitor, in Rochester for forty years, dealing mainly in crime and divorce people in stress were my stock in trade. A lifetime of saving the innocent from their just deserts, making bricks without straw, being regularly deceived by plausible rogues. They're all somewhere in these pages from the innocent schoolboy through villains and bent lawyers to Horatio Nelson and not forgetting the ladies, from the nervous bride to the well endowed and the wayward. All human life is here as a recent newspaper used to say (all safely anonymous – Don't panic Charlotte, Don't give him your name Pyke!)

In that other life I was far too busy keeping balls in the air and doing up old properties and old cars (there's a 1933 Aston in here somewhere) to find time to pen poems, but believe me it all changes when you retire – well it does for husbands – and the odd poem crept in. But six years on is it becoming an obsession? I wake up in the night to alter a line and next evening after a few Cotes du Rhones I alter it back again. Oh the joy and relief of seeing it all in print. I can't make further alterations and I'm sleeping much better thank you.

Many of my friends will recognise each other but not themselves which is as it should be. Each at peace with their little quirks. I hope I recapture in them and you a poetic interest you thought you'd lost. Don't read it all at once or you'll need counselling – it's to be savoured for the odd Idle Moment as it says on the label.

Sincere felicitations,

Godfrey Sparks

The Old Joinery
East Cross
Tenterden
Kent
TN30 6AD   June 2014

godfreysparks@aol.com

CONTENTS

4	**Introduction**
10	A Geordie's Lament
11	My England
12	Maria's Lament
13	"Would like to Meet"
14	"Dear Box 69"
15	The Rampant Rooster
16	Peggoty's Parlour
18	The Church Choir
19	Taxman Tactics
21	I'm so proud to be Brown British
23	The New Battle Hymn
25	Alice Slack R.I P.
26	The Gigolo
27	Keep Passing the Water
29	My Charlotte
30	Holy Deadlock
32	A Wild Weekend
33	Welcome Fiona
34	41 Ashford Road
35	Tony Kleine's got mine
36	Peter Michaux
37	Geoff Making R.I.P.

38	Spring
39	A Christmas Song
41	The Internet Date
42	The Sporting Voyeur
43	A Roman Holiday
45	The New Girl
46	The Wheelie Bin Man
47	A Schoolboy's Prayer
48	The Wedding Night
49	Men are All the Same
50	Lullaby
51	The Newly Elected Man
53	The Credit Crunch
55	Girl Talk
57	Jacks Final Number
59	Madeleine
61	Paranoia
62	The Departure Lounge
64	The Grandfather Clock
66	The Pudding Club
68	The Girl who went astray
70	The Office Party
72	The Bent Brief
74	Night Panic

76	The Burglar
77	Nana's Advice
79	Don't Ask me in the morning
80	Britannia Weeps
81	A Little Bit on the Side
83	My Treasure
86	"Come on Get on with it"
87	Dear Adelaide
89	Will's "The Seven Ages"
90	De Profundis
91	Brigitte's Smile
92	"I'll make my escape on the A28"
93	Brown Eyes Blue
94	Recycled Fools and Horses
95	The Night Shift
97	"If..."
99	Wrinkles don't Hurt
100	The Knock on the Door
101	Modern Verse
102	A Turkish Evening
104	The Country Walk?
105	Charity Shopping
107	The Mermaid
108	Shared Space

109	There is Still Time
110	"I bought the bloody pie from Tesco's"
111	A Family Fortune
113	Tomorrow
116	The Beginner
115	The Prodigal Husband
117	Maggie May
118	"TWIGGS"
119	The Vicar said......
120	Calais
122	The Old Millionaire
123	Dear Miss Ho
124	Salade Niçoise
125	The Wine Tasting
127	The Great War
128	The Diamond Jubilee
130	The Gurkha Soldier
131	Unnatural Selection
132	The Hills of Kandahar
134	Lord Nelson's Lament
139	Goodbye My Love

A Geordie's Lament

I come from way up North, Hinny, where they called a spade a spade
And men get bloody noses and no one's overpaid.
There's shipbuilding and steel and the hewing out of coal
And the winters last for ever and most are on the dole.

So I girded up my loins and I headed for the South
Where the sun is always shining and no one is uncouth.
I tidied up my vowels and got myself new kit
Then I queued up at the job centre and hoped my face would fit.

They offered me a railway job "You'll travel quite a lot
It's steamy in the galley and it can get bloody hot.
North Eastern line to Newcastle you'll operate from there
We'll supply your uniform so keep your suit for spare".

So now I'm back where I began – a salutary tale
No southern birds and Shepherd Neame – it's Newcastle Brown Ale.

My England

England my England don't change anymore
too much has been lost of this land I adore.
It won't be the same when the best bits are gone
I'm starting to feel I no longer belong.

Children from babies don't do as they're told
Selfish, indulged, no respect for the old
Half wait to be offered some job that they like
While they play with their iPads not get on their bike.

Pandacar'd policemen with Tazers in hand
are releasing young thugs with a mild reprimand.
All far too young to remember the time
when justice and punishment fitted the crime.

Gay clergy now lead us, their numbers are rife
Ordained, they are traitors to Christian life.
They react to their critics as if they'd been stung –
their liberal lifestyle's confusing the young.

It seems no one's to blame for our national decline –
factories are closing, no ships on the Tyne.
Those who died for this country would be horrified
Would our life <u>now</u> be worse if we'd been occupied?

Education, the Papers, T.V. are dumbed down
The country is bankrupt – with thanks Gordon Brown.
We have drunks on the streets and we blame Tony Blair –
when the last of us leaves there'll be no one to care.

Unchecked immigration – the door's open wide
The Nation's creating its own genocide.
Like a runaway train this can't carry on –
Someone put on the brakes before England is gone.

Maria's Lament

Don't sing me no more love songs dear Roberto
Don't stir me till my heart is all athrob
Don't worship me and swear that you'll be faithful
Do something useful, Get yourself a job.

I take in the village laundry and the washing
I boil it and I fold away the clothes
and all the time I hear your serenading
as I iron the sheets the sweat drips off my nose.

The queues of people waiting for their laundry
see me slaving as you sit upon your bottie
They humour me and say that I'm so lucky
to do the work and have my Pavarotti.

I've pleaded with you go and find employment
your songs of love are driving me berserk
It's killing me just keeping things together
For God's sake man just find yourself some work.

Would Like to Meet...

Dear "Fun loving male from West Kent"
Your small ad was for me Heaven sent
All the qualities listed are just what I need
(though in view of your age perhaps not guaranteed)
That it all could be mine has made me weak kneed
I adore Country Life and high fashion in tweed.

The Bentley, the farm, the weekends away
They all ring my bell like a red letter day.
Your house in the country so out of the way
Email is too slow – I can come right away.

You're seeking "a blonde who is able to fish"
At your age I suspect you'd like Lillian Gish
Well my hair I can shade to the colour you wish
And I've spent half my life trying to hook a big fish

When we've had lunch I could sit on your lap
Or wait while you have your afternoon nap
I could busy myself with some gifts to unwrap
Then we'd go for a drive in the pony and trap.

You say that you're seventy "but still feeling young"
Well I'm half your age and it's said I'm well sprung.
And as for being "fun loving, cute and laid back"
You won't know what's hit you when we hit the sack.

So I'm just what you need, I tick all the boxes
I'll help on the farm and I'll learn to shoot foxes.
There's only one problem – I'll not add any other
I know it's a bind but I'll have to bring mother.

I've started to pack so ring anytime
Your Lady in Waiting at Box 69.

Dear Box 69

Dear box 69 I regret the delay
But letters arrived by the sack full today.
Thinking things through I've been up half the night
And now I have hundreds of letters to write.

With so many offers of help on the land
I'm surprised an old farmer could be in demand.
With each letter I knew that I wasn't James Bond
And would just be a drag to a Ravishing Blonde.

Then a letter arrived from a lady you know –
Said the things that I'd listed were "childish and low"
That such aspirations "just did me no credit"
I felt so embarrassed that I'd even said it!

I'd not thought of a lady from the W.I.
Who'd been a Brown Owl and could make a game pie
All I <u>need</u> is home cooking and a cuddle or two
From a lady my age who can make rabbit stew.

We've discussed all the aspects over the phone
And your mum thinks it's better if she comes alone
So for countless more years I think I'll be content
To be your Step Father (Box 60) West Kent.

The Rampant Rooster

I am a Rampant Rooster I'm strong in wing and leg
I've laid a lot of chickens but I've never laid an egg.
I have to get up early and make an awful din
and strut about and preen myself and act all masculine.

I'd much prefer the quiet life just scratching in the sun
but as the Rampant Rooster well there's duties to be done.
I'd like to give the girls a break and say that I forgot
but if I'm spotted slacking I'll end up in the pot.

Some of you may envy me all proud and spick and span
Strutting around my harem – the farmyard Don Juan
But it's when my chicks stop laying that, speaking man to man,
Its goodbye Cock a Doodle and Hello Coc au Vin.

"Peggoty's Parlour", Rochester

In the corner of the teashop
Here I sit but not for tea
It's so noisy yet so peaceful –
All their chatter's not for me.
Secrets told across the Wedgewood
Scandal over cups of tea.
For latest wooings, Council doings
Peggoty's the place to be.

By the window sits a lady
With a silly feather hat.
The little one who does the listening
She's her sister from the chat.
There is a problem with her husband
And some female at the bank
I won't bother you with details –
Though they're both being rather frank.

All the City's gossip's here
Traded over tea and cakes.
"She's getting married for the third time –
Never learns from her mistakes!"
"Did you see those boots in Oxfam!"
"Yes, I'm sure she's on the pill"
Choice snippets bounce from wall to wall
"I'm told they've called the baby Paul."

The cathedral clock is striking
As a girl comes into view
The young man stands and smiles –
This is a lover's rendezvous.
Some scheme is planned –
They are agreed.
I look away – pretend to read.

Us eager newshounds need a break
Some place to hang the dirty mac.
Somewhere the news will come to us
While we enjoy a modest snack.
Peggoty's is that retreat –
"Retreat from what?" I hear you mock
Well from whatever I was up to –
In newshound speak "to burn some clock."

I trust I don't look too suspicious
Sitting here and all alone
My teashop brings me all the news
While I consume a buttered scone
And then perhaps a slice of gateau –
Or another piece of cake –
Gathering info makes you hungry
But it's my job for heaven's sake.

The Church Choir – Choral Conversation

Tenor: Can you shove along the pew a bit and give me breathing space
And sing a little softer you sound like Double Base.
And when you do crescendo do you have to pull a face?
And it's time you washed you surplus, it's really a disgrace.

Base: If you tightened up your braces you might reach a higher note
And then try to sing the music as you see that it was wrote.
And the congregation's tiring of looking down your throat
And your weekly observations now are getting on my goat.

Pianist: I don't know why I come here no one listens to me play
You sing as if the pianist is getting in the way –
I play a note and later on I hear a ricochet!
I <u>never</u> had this trouble with Jacqueline du Pre.

Alto: Just because you sing soprano doesn't mean you are Queen Bee.
Before you joined the choir it was always trouble free
But now your constant moaning brings on my PMT
And if something doesn't change I'll see us both in A & E.

Soprano: You shouldn't try to struggle dear with notes you cannot reach
You're in the Parish Choir not selling shellfish on the beach.
So slacken off your stays and don't try to over reach.
Oh, look out now the Vicar's here, he's going to make a speech.

Vicar: We're gathered here together in the sight of God......

Taxman Tactics

I trust that you have not been lax
and failed to pay your Income Tax.
You must always pay on time
or pay the Assessment plus a fine.
It's calculated once a year
by some faceless tax cashier
then posted to the business sector
by your local Tax Inspector.

Never lax or unobservant
is this breed of Civil Servant.
Those courses that he undertook
have taught him how to bait a hook.
He will read you like a book
however confident you look.
No trade or shop is overlooked
He can smell when the books are cooked –

So, God forbid, the dreaded spectre
you're summoned to your Tax Inspector.
Park your car two streets away.
No trace you've been on holiday.
Don't draw attention to yourself
or give the slightest sign of wealth.
Wear trousers splitting at the crotch
and never wear a ring or watch.
Some choose to don their oldest shirt
and fill their fingernails with dirt.

Your books may show a tax aversion –
but don't give him the pencil version.
All assets he will seek the source
and hope you'll say "t'was on a horse."
That reply will guarantee the anger of The Treasury.
It starts a Tax Investigation,
the third degree, intimidation.

You'd not believe what they can do.
The bastards at the Revenue.
No sweat to skin you to the bone.
They claim they can get blood from stone.
By this stage you will look the part –
say you've not been well and clutch your heart.
A fact that he will fail to mention –
He needs your tax to pay his pension.

But why ask me to give advice
my books were always imprecise
See, I have been this way before –
Is that the Bailiffs at the door?
The best advice is pay on time
and so avoid this pantomime.

"I'm so proud to be Brown British"

I'm so proud to be Brown British and to waive the Union Jack,
I started life in Mumbai but I won't be going back.
Many <u>choose</u> to live in Leicester which is known for curry smells,
But the <u>cream</u> of us Brown British make our home in Tunbridge Wells.

The Raj gave us democracy – we won't let you forget,
You did so much for India we must repay our debt.
To our Empress Queen Victoria we were the "Jewel in her Crown",
In your hour of need she knew we'd never let you down.
So half a million Indians left our homes to heed her call –
England's only tiny – you just couldn't take us all.

<u>Now</u> there's a devious English Plot thought up by Mandelson,
That if England's run down enough no more will want to come.
I've noticed serious slippage – of your exports nothing sells,
I've moaned no end about it as "Browned off of Tunbridge Wells".

You don't want Afghans or Somalis, who sneak in here by stealth,
You <u>need</u> us chaps from India – we're British Commonwealth.
We all know the National Anthem and we've come to do our best,
And once we're here we cannot wait to take our "British Test".

If the locals had to take it half would fail the British Test,
They think Churchill sold insurance and being on Benefit is best.
Most know next to nothing about basic British life –
Some thought that Queen Victoria was David Beckham's wife!

In the UK you have Temples and Mosques and holy places,
No prejudice is shown to the faiths of other races.
Most Indians are Hindu but a lot still favour Mecca,
If we can't attend by Holy Cow we go by Double Decker.

Brown British go for special jobs, for which our skills are bent,
No need to slave like blacks – there's no sugar cane in Kent.
The NHS or Civil Service – hard work I think's the key –
Some day perhaps a magistrate or even an M.P.

We don't eat greasy burgers or raw fish like the Nips,
Though I have known new arrivals have curry on their chips.
I'm here to advise them and it's my sincere wish,
They should all eat chicken tikka – the British National Dish.

I've taken trains around England – it's a green and pleasant land,
They're always overcrowded and you usually have to stand.
They say they run on time but I've yet to see the proof –
They're little better than India where we travelled on the roof.

This nonstop rain it gets me down I've lost my sense of fun,
For jolly nearly six months now I've never seen the sun.
The Lord listens to the English, who never make a fuss,
But <u>why</u> sing so heartily "Long to rain over us"?

The Queen should get a sun lamp – sometimes she looks so pale,
A bargain break in Poona is never known to fail.
When she goes to foreign parts or just pops into the town,
She'd fit in so much better in a lightish shade of brown.

The New Battle Hymn

Mine eyes have seen the Glory of the stores in Oxford Street
I'll be shopping till I'm dropping or be dying on my feet.
I've bought handbags, shoes and dresses and I haven't stopped to eat
As time is marching on.

The seven floors of Selfridges weren't made for Jimmy Choos
But that didn't stop me buying just a few more pairs of shoes
I think one pair is too tight and the rest are like canoes
But they all look really fab.

I secured my Haute Couture from a House in Portman Square
The style is just divine and I could wear it anywhere.
If we're summoned to the Palace or we dine with Tony Blair
It will blow them all away.

And a little coat from Burberry's – the price was fairy tale –
Of course it would be cheaper if I'd waited for the sale
But those horrid crowds of people they'd be fighting tooth and nail
And it might by then be gone.

"Janet Reger" lingerie is almost out of reach
Her darling little bras and pants in pink and blue and peach.
I couldn't make my mind up so I told her "Three of each"
As I know they'll earn their keep!

I always go to Aspreys if I'm in that part of Town
And I <u>might</u> disclose the price when we're beneath the eiderdown.
We'd rather spend it now than leave it all to Gordon Brown
And they wrap things with such care.

I've flashed my plastic till I've worn the numbers off the card,
If I ever get to Harrods they will say that I'm debarred
And they'll put me in a taxi and they'll send a bodyguard
As my buys need taking home.

Just pop me in the cab and send me back to Waterloo
As my husband will be waiting for a loving rendezvous.
He likes me to have fun but will he beat me black and blue
When the Bills come rolling in?

I know he won't – he likes me to look pretty!

Alice Slack R.I.P.

Here lies the body of Alice Slack
I'm sorry to say that she's not coming back.
Throughout her short life she brought comfort and joy
To many a husband and many a boy.
When you'd finished your daily grind
A girl like Alice would oft spring to mind.

She didn't cook and she didn't sew
But in what she did best she didn't half go.
You needn't hang on to every word that she said
But you had to hang on to the side of the bed!
The town is much poorer now Alice has gone
But I'm told a replacement is coming along!

Dear Alice had always held out the promise
Of years of loyal service that's now taken from us.
She's lying here now with 12 stone on her chest
And that was the weight that Alice loved best.
The happiest girl in the cemetery
Lying flat on her back for eternity.

The Gigolo

The gigolo's name was Timothy Good.
He carried his weight where a man should
Very impressive – you'd think it was wood.
There's a lot of demand for Timothy Good.

If you're inclined to get on his list
You'll wait till October – you'll think you've been missed.
Then a letter arrives through the other sort of mist
"Oh! What have I done I'm the next to be kissed!"

God, the anxiety – whether I should
Spend the housekeeping on Timothy Good,
And charging us girls – he's no Robin Hood
And making me choose between pleasure and food

I only enrolled just to show that I could
But that didn't mean that I definitely would …
You're all dying to know just where I stood
Well, he's very well named is that Timothy Good!

Keep Passing the Water

Our Recycled Drinking Water – it shouldn't make you ill
Though heavily polluted with the Contraceptive Pill.
Not good for growing lads and the reproductive train
but why address the problem, they know lads won't complain.
You haven't seen the last of it when pee goes down the drain
The Water Board soon treats it and it's out the tap again.

It's man's most basic need – Is the water fit to drink?
How many times has the same bit gone flushing down the sink?
Each time it does the rounds it's carefully diluted –
They strain it and they filter it – but the stuff is still polluted.
We <u>tell</u> lads to keep healthy – never smoke a cigarette
Then we force them to drink pee from some bird they've never met.

In the 1960s before the pill came in
Guys could face the world proud to be masculine.
Ovulating women would seek out alpha males
All contented with their manhood – though a few had ponytails.
Some girls preferred the muscular from shifts that started early
Some guys wore shoes with pointed toes but none of them were girly.

The British tribe once ruled the world our might we did unleash
from the Roast Beef of Old England not feeding men on quiche.
Kitted in their uniform they'd follow pipe and drum
Manhood meant achievement – everlasting fame for some.
But what value now has manhood – just a problem to overcome –
and a few years on this water Lord knows what you'll become.

Once we'd offer girls our seats – they'd smile, their hearts would throb
But now it's thought more courteous to offer them your job.
Testosterones being diluted, our youth are being neutered
And into the ranks of "modern man" they're furtively recruited.
You'll see them any evening pushing a shopping trolley –
The smart suburban housewife followed by her wally.

We're all onto recycling, it's not a handicap,
But for God's sake only packaging not water from the tap.
Avoid the filthy stuff, it's poisoning the nation –
For little boys, the sensitive, it's chemical castration.
The time's now overdue for MALE emancipation
Does there <u>have</u> to be a crisis before some action's taken?

A THIRD of our drinking water is recycled sewage.
We're getting the benefit of our neighbour's medication – Statins, Viagra, Heroin, and female synthetic hormones that the present filter system cannot reach.
A Poet's Revolt is overdue!

My Charlotte

I have a friend called Charlotte I've known her many years
We've been through much together in happiness and tears.
She was a sport at Roedean, the captain of lacrosse
And later with the Tickham Hunt – a fine seat in a horse.

It started off quite jolly – just a giggle and a hoot
But you know how it goes once you taste forbidden fruit.
She got in Prince Andrew's set – lots of golf and Pimms
And later on a snort or two and other frightful things.

She'd lots of racy friends then and a flat in Beauchamp Place
Where she'd sometimes drop her undies, but she'd never drop an 'H'.
I popped to London twice a week no matter what the weather -
She had a chum called Mandy and the two worked well together!

Happy days were spent between satin sheets in Town
But now that I've retired it's time to settle down.
I'll always remember all the moans and sighs
And when the storm was over how I'd sleep between her thighs.

I never thought the time would come to let my Charlotte go
And for some other lucky guy to call and say "Hello".
But my ticker isn't helping and my vigour's nearly spent
And Beauchamp Place is pricy and I can't afford the rent.

She's still a sporting girl who'd be mostly loyal and true
And frankly I was hoping I could pass her on to you!

Holy Deadlock – or advice to young men contemplating wedlock

I'm sitting in this Hostel for men who've been thrown out
And with our crazy system there's now more of us about.
Marriage vows are personal things when all is said and done
And "Just one size fits all" won't do for everyone.

I've checked my married friends out – I know the mess they're in
Most should have played the field then settled down in sin.
The marriage stakes are pretty high – you're on a single number
And it comes up one in twenty or less I shouldn't wonder.

No guy at the Races picks a young mare with no form
But in The Matrimonial Stakes that seems to be the norm.
Why rush in and put your shirt on a pretty filly
Then try to walk a tightrope and not do anything silly?

The Conjugal Knot's worn round the neck to remind you of your vows
It's supposed to stop you wandering off – like a bell on cows.
Then if you go philandering the outcome will be grim
It's great to walk on water but not if you can't swim.

Morning suits and champers or a hog roast in the Hall?
Why choose to be the roasted hog or the fall guy at the Ball?
Everybody cheers as you board the marriage hearse
But once the door's slammed shut you could be off to somewhere worse.

Young men just seeking fun get pushed around and harried
They mumble a few words in church and suddenly they're married.
Come back from the pub some night a few pints for the worse
Mumble a few words in bed and bang – it's a divorce!

It can easily happen – this advice is for the best
The wife gets nearly everything – her lawyers get the rest.
The truth of modern marriage in old Mick Jagger's nouse
Is "You find a woman you don't like and buy the cow a house".

But if you live together and she keeps her maiden name
She'll be just as beautiful and you can stay the same.
And when the boat starts leaking as I know it will
You'll try hard to patch it up and she'll try harder still.

So don't rush your matrimonials for the cooking or the pleasure
Or you could soon be heading here where we all repent at leisure.
When Eve was in the Garden she didn't plight her troth
She gave her man an apple and then they had it off.

This Guidance is well intentioned so treat it like the Gospel
Or do the same as we did and join us at the Hostel!

A Wild Weekend

The wife's gone to her mother's, the sun is shining bright
So it's golf or read the papers and will I get stoned tonight?
Oh yes I know I'll miss her – I'll think that I've gone deaf.
And she'll worry that I'm aimless, that I'll be bored to death.

I won't say that I'm a tomcat, that I might go astray,
But no pussy in the parlour – this mouse is going to play.
I've found my old address book, I'll start with letter A
"It's been a long time Annie – can you come out to play?"

Oh God it sounds pathetic – at my age its passé –
The lover's lane we knew so well is now a motorway.
Then halfway through that hallowed book I reached the letter K
Oh what a little raver, what will she have to say?

Lucky I kept her number, I'll ring up "Crashed out Kate"
The wildest of the old gang she'll not turn down a date.
"Oh, hi there, this is Rambo, can I speak to Kate?"
"My aunt's a Reverend Mother – you're twenty years too late!"

I used to be so active but now I don't know how
If I'd joined the Foreign Legion they'd have thrown me out by now.
I must be very careful or this weekend's going to drag –
To "should I dig the garden or should I wash the Jag?"

That's car wheels on the gravel! – it's the wife I apprehend
"I've only been to Tesco's – it's my mother's next weekend"
"Oh yes, I'm sure you told me – I'd wondered what to do –
We should see her more often so I'll come along with you."

Welcome Fiona!

Oh Dear, what can the matter be
Word's leaked out we've a Lady in Rotary
Came as a shock but not a catastrophe
Once we got used to the change.

Just one lady member's no problem numerical
All on her own so don't get hysterical
Ticks all the boxes except for the spherical
Pleasure to have her aboard.

That girls choose to join us is really a compliment
Lets go the whole way and vote her as President
Doubt if she'd do it – she's far too intelligent –
Thought we could give it a try...

The Old Brigade are like rooks in a rookery
Squarking on about knitting and cookery
Hardly a problem they'd sleep through it anyway
Gives them the joy of a moan.

Professional girls are not an anomaly
Bound to join in by the Laws of Biology
One at a time and then ever more frequently –
After you Dick with the frock!

41 Ashford Road

The flowers in Mike's garden are disciplined and loyal,
They flower all the summer. They don't moan about the soil.
If they're feeling thirsty they're content to wait for rain.
I'm told that every year it's always been the same.
He lays out on his day bed – when he smiles at them they bloom,
And if the wind blows through them they sing to him in tune.

So why is it my garden is like a battleground,
With resentful little flowers and dead and dying all around?
The ones that are alive seem truculent and idle –
Some might hang in one more year but most are suicidal.

They seem to welcome pests and show them where to hide
And I fight back with DDT and squirt insecticide.
But the battle's nearly over – we've decided this October
To dig the blighters up and slab the whole lot over.

Tony Klein's got mine!

A financial adviser named Klein
Said "I'll care for your money like mine"
Well that's what he said, kept it under his bed,
With hindsight that should have been fine.

Then he said:-
If you want interest or gain
And can take some worry and strain,
Forget the Footsie or Bourse
And I'll put the lot on a horse".

So:-
He put it on Lightning at 7 to 1
And she came in second and it was all gone.
Financial Advisors give no guarantee
Except in the small print that they'll take a fee

But:-
The Steward's Enquiry cancelled the win, so
Lightening moved up one and the money rolled in,
But the strain was too much it just went to my head,
So all of my winnings stay under his bed!

Peter Michaux

Peter Michaux's really old
He's 99 or so I'm told.
When he was born the earth was flat
And for some time it stayed like that.

Nowadays our life's much calmer
In Peter's day young men wore armour.
Damsels then were all about
And Knightly Peter helped them out.

Peter's calling was the Navy
Cobalt blue and very wavy.
Fought with Drake in the Spanish Main
And luckily came home again.

Then to Chatham – joined Lord Nelson
Gave the French a bloody lesson.
The Frogs could cope with any foe
Except the Admiral and Michaux.

We see him next on Russian convoys
With guns and tanks for Stalin's boys.
High on the bridge in his duffle coat
Looking out for the lone "U" boat.

Now had his fill of wars and peaces
He holidays in Spain and Greeces
An English Oak that never withers
Peter Michaux is still with us.

Geoff Making RIP

The next guy I see through my lens
Is a chap in the Making of pens.
They used to be in packets of three
But now they're in boxes of tens.

We all love gentleman Geoff
One of the kindest of mens
If you give him the wink
He'll keep buying you drink
If you've bought one of his pens!

A philosopher down to his kneecaps
He's wont to observe now and then
"If you haven't got lead in your pencil
Then make sure you've got ink in your pen"

If he gives you a cheque for your troubles
Just pay it in pretty Quink
Or the words they will all disappear
As he uses invisible ink!

If you're sending a note to your dear one
Don't click it out on a Dell
Unscrew the cap of your old Conway Stewart
Or a Parker will do just as well.

His inks you can buy in all colours
Navy Blue's the best colour for pens
Geoff's researched colours quite closely
It's the same as the knickers of WRNS.

We go to "White Gables" for meetings
And all sit outside if it's hotter
Where he'll give you a drink and a bottle of Quink
And a packet of things for your blotter.

Spring

I wandered aimlessly along
Passed Pub and Bar and Coffee Shop
When all at once I came upon
A host of Rotary Crocuses.
Beside the road beneath the trees
A purple carpet in the breeze.

They stretched in a never ending bed
Towards the West where the footpath led.
No poet I know could not be gay,
To see such beauty on the way –
And others coming out the Pub,
They smiled and thanked the Rotary Club.

Such thoughtfulness and effort shows
As every year that carpet grows.
Now oft when on my couch I lie
That picture comes to my mind's eye
And oh my heart with pleasure fills
For crocuses not daffodils.

A Christmas Song   -To be sung with Gusto and Harvey's Best

Oh little town of Tenterden
How much we owe to thee
Those from afar and those born here
Shall ever grateful be.

O'er hill and dale the Christmas Sale
Is just about to start
When choir boys sing and cash till ring
Get in and be a part.
Get in, get in, get in,
Get in and be a part!

At Waitrose and at Te-e-e-esco's
The "Big Issue" is sold
And they're stocked out and all about
There's gifts for young and old.

There's oh so much the French and Dutch
Come here to spend a bomb
So keep it up! Oh keep it up!
And long may it go on.

With Christmas lights and wondrous sights
The town is really humming
But hide your girls, switch off your lights,
The Rotary Club are coming.

With tabards on and rosy cheeks
They make a cheerful sight.
The hopes and fears of some old dears
Are realised tonight!

It's White's for jewels and Webb's for tools
They're both along the street.
And Jones for plants and Swaines for pants
And lots of things for feet.

Perhaps a steam train down the line
Along the railway track.
It takes you from our little town
And usually brings you back.

How silently, how silently
The Traffic Wardens come
And they give out a Fixed Account
To every dad and mum.

No ear may hear their coming
But in the High Street still
If shoppers stay too long well they
Receive a sort of bill.

A beacon is the Tent' den Club
Which is now where I am
Where old men weep into their beer
And young men chat up Sam.

No Cinema or Bingo Hall
Just trees and pubs and beer.
It's country walks and early nights
And little crime to fear.

While mortals sleep the Councils keep
An ever watchful eye
At thirty feet all down the street
There's cameras in the sky.

Oh! Little Town, Jewel of the Weald
We're proud as you can tell.
Good God we'd choose no other place
O' Lord Emmanuel.

The Internet Date

I put my details on the web – non smoker, Scorpio
And added a nice photo from about ten years ago
Selective information – but all he'd need to know
And I waited for an email from my website Romeo.

His reply was pretty rapid – hot flush and all aglow –
He said his name was Nigel, I told him mine was Flo.
We agreed on a place in the High Street where I knew the lights were low
And looked forward to a steak and a large glass of Bordeaux.

I was in full battle dress as you would for such a date
Expecting a nice local chap whom I could detonate.
Then Nigel appeared from the shadows – I swear he was 6ft 8
I saw hairy arms and a big gold chain and his ear rings vibrate.

No doubt the steak would be lovely but I'm sure I'd be the dessert
So a quick change of plan was essential to stop some silly girl getting hurt.
I blurted my nose had gone shiny – to the ladies I had to divert
A quick cross of the floor and out the rear door
I was down the back lane in a spurt.

My friends were all full of advice
And yes, I am truly indebted
"Flo, You've left it too late for an Internet Date –
Try Rotarians! – You know they've been vetted!"

The Sporting Voyeur

There is a time for dreaming and a time to be poetic
But Summer is the time to be Vicariously Athletic
I settle in the <u>Armchair</u> put aside my Keats and Shelley
It's now July, the time has come for tennis on the telly.

Its true I might nod off and rest my feet on Rover
To dream I'm in another age where I am Casanova
But <u>not</u> when SHE is playing and <u>not</u> till it's all over
The Style, The Skill, The Legs, The Grunts – Maria Sharapova

From my <u>Deck Chair</u> by the green I watch the Village Cricket
I never miss the ladies match – oh how they guard their wicket.
Their cries of "Well played Smithy!" or "Jones to Extra Cover"
None would guess their Captain is our G.P. and a mother.

A sunny day, a little breeze, so British and serene
At four the stumps are pulled for tea – Its strawberries and cream.
It's when the game is over that some young men discover
Her girls are well protected – each wears a "manhole cover".

I place my <u>Beach Chair</u> in the sand along the Cote d'Azur
The sun the sea the little waves the coastal curvature.
The cries of girls cavorting awake me from my dozes –
Five hundred topless beauties, a thousand puppies noses.

A lovely girl then heads my way in a shocking pink bikini
Behind my shades my eyes are wide, my ears can hear Puccini.
If I am now in Wonderland then up should pop my Genie
And first I'll choose the blonde in pink and then a Lamborghini.

A Roman Holiday

I'm sitting here alone in the Coliseum in Rome
Nowhere could be better to pen a noble poem.
The evening sun is setting as the stones give out their heat
Everything is perfect, except for my poor feet.

These bargain basement weekends look fine in t' Daily Mail
But when you get to foreign parts, well that's another tale.
The pensioni's by the station – they want you to stay out
The star rating was done at night when no stars were about.
Every meal's spaghetti with various sorts of bean
I used to like spaghetti but I'll not eat it again.

The tour rep she booked the Guide – but only for one day.
One day to see the whole damn place, there was no other way.
We met outside the Vatican for our La Dolce Vita
Then everyone inside to see the statue of St Peter.

(Some Italian nuns with their rosary beads
Atone for their President's sinful deeds.
With all those models brazen and tarty
And secretly wish they'd been at the party!)

We all streamed down the central aisle – no loitering in the pews
The guide was used to bargain tours and she wore training shoes.
The Sistine Chapel came and went in a sort of a blur
And then through lots of cloisters – we'd no idea where we were.
She told us to get money out for the Trevi Fountain
Then herded us up some Spanish steps like climbing up a mountain.

Rome bristles with reminders of its imperial past
But nothing really sticks when you're covering it so fast.
The non-stop Michael Angelo – I've got cultural indigestion
God knows how he found the time but that's another question.

It's Michael this and Michael that for every dome and steeple
If they get too pushy, well you can go off people.
He was a clever chap and the Romans love him dear
But now I've had enough of Mike – right up to here!

Lord Byron had a lovely time – he lived here for years
But I'm told he came privately and not with Cosmos Tours.
Some capers he got up to I know weren't very nice
But that's not our problem – it's not included in the price.

Many were lost along the way – some longing for their homes
The last time I saw the wife was in the Catacombs.
My poetic mood has gone – my Roman ode will go unwritten
But I'll take up my pen again when I get back to Britain.

A poem about Sheerness docks I guess is pretty rare
Where Michael Angelo played no part so far as I'm aware.
There must be inspiration among the jetties and the pier
And I can break off anytime for a sani and a beer.
Sitting by the dockside I'm sure my thoughts will flow
And it should be pretty quiet as the wife won't want to go.

The New Girl   (if only!)

The New Girl in the flat next door
Has disco parties until four.
Don't think she ever hits the sack –
My 45's jump off their track.

I rang her bell to say my bit
"Oh neighbour come right in,
I'll fix a stiff one – scotch or gin?"
Well yes, I did submit.

As pretty as a Diamond Flush
I gazed into her eyes.
She said "Your hands are round my thighs
My, you are in a rush!"

Her Botox lips were shaped for sin
Her chassis shaped for action,
Clothed in Lurex leopard skin
For total satisfaction.

Was it love or was it lust?
An issue quite concerning
Some other time to be discussed –
Not when my fuse was burning!

Now twice a week I do complain
And her warm welcome is the same.
I've never asked the New Girl's name
And she still calls me Neighbour.

The Wheelie Bin Man

"I'm from the council, lady, I must know where's your bin
I calls here every Tuesday and I never finds you in".
"The councils very nosy – is that why I pay my tax
It used to be for bin men to take away my sacks –

Well I've just come back from Tesco's with a couple of pork chops
And to be honest sir I've been looking in the shops"
"Look lady I don't need to know which one's you went in
I only need to know where's your wheelie bin"

"Well before that I went to Boots for some very soothing cream
I can highly recommend it if you must know where I've been"
"I don't need any cream lady in a jar or in a tin
I just want you to tell me where's your wheelie bin"

"Oh! You must mean for my holidays with Saga Tours to Rome
When you called for your survey that's why we weren't at home
I could find you their brochure but it's in my wheelie bin
Now we're all spent up we're back to eating in –

Last night we had fish & chips so it might be a bit smelly
Both sat in the living room – watched Poirot on the telly"

"I'll take your brochure lady – just lead me to the smell
And while I'm round the back I'll take your wheelie bin as well!

A Schoolboy's Prayer

As I kneel at the foot of my bed
Many strange thoughts come into my head.
All is not fair in this world you created
Unfair advantage is taken for granted.

What has a mouse ever done to a cat
Why do you Lord let it treat it like that?
I love to see lambs in a field with their mother
Happy with her and wanting no other
And just then an eagle swoops down through the air
Surely you see that it just isn't fair.

They teach us at school that the Lord up above
Smiles down on us all with kindness and love
What sort of kindness is it to a goose
To be killed by a fox the first time it gets loose.

Lions and tigers need something to eat
But why should a little gazelle be their meat.
Of grass eating animals there are quite but a few
Wouldn't it be better if they did that too?

You kindly supplied all the grass and the trees
But why then add to it those bad allergies
The ideas were great but it wasn't a must
That they came with a load of pollen and dust.

It's not that I want to alter creation
But so many things do need big variation.
The world will soon end with a nuclear blast
And of all generations I'm told we're the last.

I know it's not easy to be right the first time
You should see some of the homework of mine.
But next time dear Lord could you try a bit harder!
And Oh! I forgot bless mother and father.   Amen.

The Wedding Night

The church bells have stopped ringing and the vicars gone to bed
And I'm just lying here as things go through my head.
The wedding day was wonderful and went without a hitch
But I know Desmond's nervous cos he's got his nervous twitch.

I've got to keep him calm or his nose will start to bleed
And on your wedding night that isn't what you need.
I'll chat on about Chelsea – but nothing really deep
And I mustn't mention Gillingham or we'll both nod off to sleep.

Everyone is nervous on their first wedding night
Mother says "Don't panic as penis's don't bite".
Well I've read every young bride's book that ever has been written
And I'm sure I've read of silly girls that really have been bitten!

But Desmond's been so kind I think he'll know what to do
Though he's not had much experience (just between me and you)
He Said "Ignore the books – they're only a load of hype –
When all is said and done it's just a water pipe".

It isn't that I'm nervous but I must know where it goes
And to be on the safe side I've tied my nighty to my toes.
Whatever comes between us might frighten me at first
But I'm sure that by the morning I'll have got over the worst.

Oh! It's all been too much for my poor Desmond
He's given up the day without a fight.
He's lying here and sleeping like a baby
Perhaps we'll try again tomorrow night.

God knows he's had all week if he thought he needed rest
It's not what I expected in my matrimonial nest.
Waking him is risky – I admit to feeling frisky
But I suppose a good night's sleep is for the best.

Men are all the same!

Some chaps think it's great to be rich,
To be cool and keep up with the trends.
But riches and looks don't matter a jot,
All a guy really needs is girlfriends.

It helps to have one or two muscles,
And girls always like a nice bum,
You mustn't be hairy or sweaty,
Or have too much flab on your tum.

Make sure your safe when you "do it",
Put on a condom that fits.
Some girls prefer ones that glow in the dark,
With the slippery knobbly bits.

She'll want you to make love an art,
And try to keep going till morning.
But usually you'll find you'll roll over and fart
When you've finished the job – and start snoring.

Lullaby

Rock a bye baby, keep your eyes closed
Daddy's gone boozing down at "The Rose".
I'd have been with him then you came along
Now I'm stuck here with my Rock a bye song.

You'd still be an angel if all'd gone to plan
I'd be down "The Rose" and supporting my man.
Mind having a baby was down on our list
Of jobs to be started but not when I'm pissed!

We wanted you badly but you were too quick
With so many vodkas I should have been sick.
I woke up next morning oh! I'd had my fill
We both blame the drink I'd forgotten my pill.

That noise in the hall means daddy's come back
His turn to take over while I hit the sack.
But just half an hour and your eyes open wide
You always seem hungry for five minutes each side.

Since you came along there's been so much to do
And most of the jobs seem to revolve around you.
With such a small family there's only us three
With two on the bottle that only leaves me.

So give me a break pal
Just for tonight
Keep your eyes closed and
Sleep on till it's light.

The Newly Elected Man
From The Palace of Westminster 2009

My Dear Father,
Your letter was in my "In Tray" when I got back to town
We'd been to Abi Dhabi sourcing loans for Gordon Brown.
Now you've got a famous son don't expect me to be here
I'll be jetting round the globe for the best part of the year
Never in one place for long – a proper Peter Pan –
You mustn't be too available when you're an elected man.

My lovely flat in Chelsea is paid for by the State
It needs to be convenient as sometimes we vote late.
I've a Jaguar and a chauffeur – he's really hale and hearty
In fact I don't need either but I can't let down the party
The housekeeper and manservant keep me spick and span -
You've got to look the part when you're an elected man.

I have a special seat – you can see it on TV
It's beautiful green leather but you won't often see me.
We do a lot of fact finding and then write short reports
Usually in the First Class lounge at foreign airports.
They lay on a special plane if there's a travel ban -
The voters like you well informed when you're an elected man.

Everything is claimed for from a kettle to a cup
I mustn't claim too little or it shows the others up.
Expenses can be tricky but I'm catching on quite quick
There's lots of chaps to help me and keep me out the nic!
It's very bad publicity if you finish in the pen – but
We all support each other as true elected men.

For promotion it would help if I was lesbian or queer –
Or a Doctorate in Scottish – there's different rules up here.
I'm living off expenses and banking all my pay
I plan to have a pretty pile by next Election Day.
I used to bank with Barclay's in High Street Tenterden
But now it's numbered Swiss accounts just for elected men.

I'm paired with a really nice bloke and we get on just fine
I vote to cancel his vote and he votes to cancel mine.
If the little people knew what really went on here
There'd be riots in the street and big trouble I fear
But it's all hushed up quite quickly – it's catch me if you can
Some questions you don't ask of an elected man.

The Palace of Westminster is thought a sober place
For erudite discussions about the human race.
But there's very serious drinking in the clubs and the societies
It should relocate to Leicester Square as "Palace of Varieties".
It's all up on the notice board – all the where's and when
And free tickets for all the shows just for elected men.

It's been said by low comedians who are usually round the bend
That we're the biggest, the longest running farce in the West End.
But it's just silly jealousy – a lot of cock and hen
You soon thicken up your skin when you're elected men.

I'm careful who I mix with – there're some dreadful rogues up here
With bookmakers and mistresses and even worse I fear.
I've no wish to go clubbing to a brothel or a den
Some think that they can walk on water once they're elected men.

I'll post this in the Commons Box where everything is free –
It doesn't work the other way when it's from you to me.
The common people question this – say it's another scam
But you never pay anything when you're an elected man

Mother always said, "Don't run before you walk"
But now I'm into pressing flesh and lots of clever talk.
I'm sorting little jobs to do in Italy and Spain,
And gradually I hope to join the Euro gravy train.
The perks are just amazing – I'll make it if I can
And then do even more good as an unelected man.
Best Wishes
Sebastian   xx

P.S. My secretary does all my post and even adds Best Wishes
She puts it in my pending tray and I just add the kisses.

The Credit Crunch

Our savings have all gone and we're living on the edge
We took them out of Nationwide and put them in a Hedge.
I'm sitting in the park – poor as a church mouse
Just waiting for the day when the council take the house.
We're all now pretty scruffy – an ugly looking bunch
But they haven't stopped us yet from doing the Credit Crunch.

For Pete's sake dancing's free so don't start getting queasy
The steps are really simple – easy and peasy.
One step forward two steps back shake your fist and moan
I'll help you one more time and then you're on your own.
So it's one step forward two steps back shake your fist and moan
And that's all you'll have left when you've lost your home.

I've long since ditched the car and now I'm on my bike
And mother's got a shopping trolley fastened to her trike.
My sister's halved her prices if she's your cup of tea
Now she'll take on anyone – well anyone but me!
My brother's in the garden shed distilling nettle punch
That'll get us going when we do the Credit Crunch.

Granny's in the kitchen but nothing's on the boil
They've cut off the electric and there's no cooking oil.
Dad's just gone bananas – he's nearly on the brink
From queuing at the fountain just to get a drink
The kids are in the garden, a really happy bunch,
Charging up and down and doing the Credit Crunch.

We've all gone to the dogs – the nation's in a hole
Some immigrants are working but the rest are on the dole.
The government have lost it and I have got a hunch
That by the time they find it we'll have cracked the Credit Crunch.

It started in the city among the towers and bells
But the Credit Crunch is national if it's reached Tunbridge Wells.
You can't pick out the bankers now cos they have ditched their togs,
And I've heard in the Medway towns blind men have sold their dogs.

Don't forget to shake your fist and don't forget to moan
And just hang on for dear life we're all now on our own.
Things are getting desperate – you can really feel the heat
When 30 million of us shake our fists at Downing Street.
They'll feel the vibrations as they sit down to lunch
Of half the bloody nation doing the Credit Crunch.

They must know our anger as they fiddle their expenses
The nations on the march – they'd better look to their defences.
They're all a load of Charlatans – it's time for kick and punch
And we'll dance on the lot of them while doing the Credit Crunch Oi!

Girl Talk

Us Big Girls we soon get to know
not to have too much cleavage on show.
Our décolleté can shock and dismay
so there's only so far you can go.

You may think me a Goddess zipped up in my bodice
but I know if my neckline's too low
I could start divorces or frighten the horses
Or cause Pacemaker fuses to blow.

Some girls are blessed to have a big chest
and others have different skills.
My blessing is mammary, it runs in the family
all the town knows my Brazils.

At the Blooming of Spring, oh the joy that they bring
when I first put my bosom on show.
Two jugs with no handle, the shock and the scandal
if I pull my tee-shirt too low.

I could give you a lecture on my architecture
and the problems I have with support
or a short seminar on the work of the bra
and the hundreds of styles that I've bought.

I've tried every shape in satin and crêpe
and I'll tell you there's one thing worth knowing
It might look like a gift but with too much uplift
I find I can't see where I'm going

I left off my vest, got a chill on my chest
and finished up croaky and wheezy.
Dad who's a cynic said "Go to the clinic,
You've seen Doc before and it's easy".

I wasn't much better, I lifted my sweater
for the medic to check on them both.
(Pause) In that stethoscopic setting I saw the doctor sweating
And I heard him use a Hippocratic Oath.

It's the extra large size that causes surprise
and it gives me great pleasure to know.
That my bust causes smiles and some men it beguiles
when I have my assets on show.

The British Heart Foundation does good across the Nation
and they tell me that I'm now their top fundraiser.
I'm not a girl who brags but I'll shift a tray and flags
When I'm buttoned up and bursting out my blazer.

Well I think that's enough, just a chat off the cuff
and <u>I know</u> why you stopped me to talk.
Now the sun has come out and there's guys all about
so I'm taking my tits for a walk.

Jack's Final Number

I'm a very old musician of the ilk of Acker Bilk,
They're calling me to play my final tune,
I'm ready for the journey – I know it will be soon
And my clarinets go with me wrapped in silk.

I've been a sessions man from the UK to Japan,
I only played the bands that stirred the soul,
That brought tears to the eyes of the toughest of G.I.s,
To make lovers cling together was my goal.

I've played in times long past with Johnnie Dankworth & James Last,
Billy Cotton, Quincy Jones – I was welcome in their homes,
But they have all moved on and the bands they had have gone,
Now I'm "The Stranger on the Shore" who will shortly be no more.

They voted my "Blue Moon" as the lover's favourite tune,
My "Bridge over Troubled Waters" could charm away your daughters,
No sweetheart could demur when she heard my "Petite Fleur",
When I muted my "Moon River" I could make a convent shiver.

The shops no longer sell my beautiful "Michelle",
And I'm told that even rarer is my haunting "Buona Sera",
If you call at HMV they've still got lovely tunes by me,
Words you can understand and with the backing of the band.

Bands your parents did adore on T.V. and Radio 4,
With Patsy Kline and Billy Jo – is it all so long ago?
It's hardly ever played – "The Moonlight Serenade",
Does no one love a ballad anymore?

When I close my eyes I can hear the other guys,
"Still playing Jack", they call – "Now you're playing for us all"
If they're in The Better Place they should love my "Amazing Grace",
Or John Denver's "Annies Song" for the guys who've all passed on.

When we played "The Way We Were" with the strings and with the brass,
I never thought those words would ever come to pass,
But one by one they left the band with just the shaking of the hand,
Such a lovely group of men – you'll never hear their like again.

My body's in extremis – just my reeds are still in tune,
I hear the distant trumpets – now I know my call is soon.

"It's been a long time Jack – the boys are <u>glad</u> to have you back,
We've had enough of harp duets – we need more <u>saxe</u> and clarinets".
"They're getting really big in Heaven –
We've lined you up with "The Temperance Seven",
All wait at The Pearly Gate – be first to hear "The Temperance Eight"!

"For celestial rhythm and blues kindly form angelic queues –
Any angels without harps to audition for our flats and sharps.
We'll soon get those heavenly feet stamping out a ragtime beat,
Now we'll put on such a show they'll probably hear us down below!"

A modest tribute to Jack Ody (1907 – 2001)

Madeleine (Year 9)

The boy I'm going to marry will be strong and tall and rich
And our wedding will be wonderful and go without a hitch.
His parents will smile at me and say I'm heaven sent
And then we'll set up home in a manor house in Kent.

I know I'll marry really well, there's no point in being coy
And somewhere in the world right now there is this yummy boy.
Perhaps just come off the cricket pitch after bowling or batting
But in another hour or so he'll have his head down swatting.

He could be studying history in London, Rome or Venice
Or just got back to college having thrashed someone at tennis.
After all the excercise and all that history
I know that he'll start thinking of a girl like me.

In all his exams he'll get an amazing grade
And perhaps the sword of honour in some military parade.
He's got to be ambitious and not just drift through life
And when he sees my CV he'll want me as his wife.

He's going to get a modern girl, perhaps he already knows,
Who'd choose a red Ferrari before a perfect rose.
I know I'm aiming pretty high but surely you see
That some girl's going to marry him so it might as well be me.

Although I'm still a teenager I can make my plans
You've gathered I want a special guy, not the also – rans.
It's strange that I half know him yet I don't know his name
And when he dreams of me it must be just the same.

Throughout all my life I'll keep my body trim
Partly cos I like too but mainly it's for him.
Cakes and sweets are out and no ifs and buts
And definitely MacDonald's – I'll eat fruit and nuts.

As too my statistics, I know my size precisely
A quick glance in the mirror – I'm coming on quite nicely!
I'll keep on with athletics and so stay lithe and supple
So later on I'll hear it said "They make a lovely couple".

I'm sure he'll love his music and have a clarinet
Then we can play together – we'll make a great duet.
Perhaps a work by Schubert of whom I'm very fond –
A shared interest in music makes a very special bond.

Just the way I look at him everyone will see
That I'll be so proud of him – and he'll be proud of me.
So maybe just around the corner or in another land
Is the boy I'm going to marry and to whom I'll give my hand.

We've never met each other, or if so he didn't say
The future's so mysterious – yet there's no other way.
They say that love is blind and that he'll take my hand to kiss
But a Knight in Shining Armour is pretty hard to miss!

Paranoia

There's a spy in my street – I know that it's true
I've seen funny parcels of wires and glue.
When I go to the shops to get coffee and tea
I see weird men and they're looking at me.

Something's going to happen – I think it's tonight
They'll create a diversion like a row or a fight
And then they'll take over and call it a coup
The terrified victims will be me and you.

They'll blow up my home every saucer and cup
And they'll kidnap the children and lock them all up
And like villains have done throughout all history
They'll murder my husband and do things to me!

Don't phone the police because they're in on it too
Oh! God help Britannia – we're all in the poo…

The Departure Lounge

Word was bound to leak out that I'm breathing my last,
Though only a rumour – such news travels fast.
Well today is the day, I've made my arrangements,
I'm paid up to date and I've cancelled engagements.

The plans that I've made weren't set up in haste.
I find Current Reality's not to my taste.
It isn't a choice that I've made off the cuff,
I've thought for some time that I've just had enough.

I plan to switch off very shortly you see –
By the time you read this it's a fait accompli.
You might spot some malaise but I'm really not ill,
The Lord hasn't called me – I've just had my fill.

I've settled old scores and paid my last bill
And under my socks you will find my Last Will.
There's one or two jobs that I'd still got to do
And some of the urgent I'm leaving to you.

I've faced the same grief, disappointment and lies
And have all the regrets as when any man dies.
The friends I've let down and the promises broken,
I should have done more when I just did a token.

I'll soon have my cloud with its heavenly view,
(There'll be lots of us there but I'll keep space for you)
I might be remembered by girls that I've kissed,
But give it a month and I'll never be missed.

At my funeral you'll be told of a man you never knew,
"The most loving, kind and talented – one of so very few..."
Mind no one thought to tell me that's the cruel paradox,
But check that it's my funeral – read the label on the box.

Oh I've had my moments in a pretty long life,
But shortly I'm done with its trouble and strife.
You'd think "Terminal Pills" would be quite hard to get,
But it's easy as pie on the Internet.

Damn it, now my tea's gone cold – it said "with a warm drink"
Such instructions to be followed to the letter I should think.
I'll pop down and make another cup
And put away the washing up,
And check the draw for the FA Cup –,
And perhaps a final tidy up?

The T.V.'s still on for the golf and the cricket,
I was going to look for my Lottery Ticket.
Living alone there's so much to do,
There's definitely more than when there were two.

My Premium Bond cheques should arrive any day,
Though I'm starting to think that most go astray –
Perhaps a weekend away with – You Know Who
Or a Singles Cruise on the QM2?

Now the sun's come out – let Heaven wait –,
Though I'll check the pills for the sell by date.
Are you sure about Heavenly Bliss unsurpassed
when this fever called living is over at last?

The Grandfather Clock

The Grandfather Clock on the landing
Is ticking my life away.
He was ticking before I could tell the time
And he's ticking the same today.
The dial reads "Tempus Fugit – 1773"
Louis was King of the French then
And his fate he couldn't foresee.

When the weights were first hung on the catgut
And the pendulum started to swing
The first tea was arriving from China
With little tea bowls from Nanking.

The Americans then were colonials,
Twas the year of the Boston Tea,
A refusal to pay British Taxes
And planning to be Tax Free.
He's witnessed our family's losses
Through battle and riot and bomb
He's stayed straight backed and impassive
Through the Crimea and Boar War and Somme.

The Head of the household still winds him
At the same time every week
And the living and dying regard him
And no less now because he's antique.
He still stands in the corner and watches
Those things you don't want to be seen
But he never asks any questions
Like "It's late and where have you been?"

And two hundred years from now
He could still be chiming in tune
When people are living in shuttles
And with houses for sale on the Moon.

There'll be little time then for his ticking
And they won't want chiming in space.
They'll say that he's just a dust gatherer
And that old things are now out of place.
They'll take him away from his family –
He'll be far too brave to cry –
And they'll line him up with the other old clocks
and they'll leave him there to die.

The Pudding Club

I <u>am</u> a rotten gambler, I <u>know</u> I should convert
To someone who just watches as I always lose my shirt.
I've kept the bookies children – don't be too quick to condemn
Somehow the horses get to know I've put my shirt on them.

Fast women and slow horses, I could never get it right.
My dog's the one that stops to pee and the rest are out of sight.
I know I drink too much – I always seem so dry,
Just take me to a brewery and leave me there to die.

A friend of mine who's been around
And whose advice is usually sound said
"At <u>your</u> age you must abandon the Vices of Beelzebub.
Change your ways while you still can
And join your local Pudding Club".

Now my past is all behind me – I have joined a Pudding Club.
Each week I now pick winners but in the form of grub.
The Germans make fine Strudel and the French are good at Tart,
But the Steaming British Puddings found its way into my heart.

We meet up every Tuesday down at the Coach & Horses
For blissful British Puddings and magic steaming sauces.
As with any club of merit there's a certain protocol –
No word is <u>ever</u> uttered like angina or cholesterol.

Don't ask me all the pudding names you'll only get me flustered.
I always start with Treacle Sponge which comes with lumpy Custard.
Their lowly Rolly Polly is pretty hard to lick
Or the oral gratification of a British Spotted Dick.

Each week I choose a taster from the puddings on the list
Then if they're to my liking I do an Oliver Twist.
It's anybody's guess what they put in Eton Mess
But those dreamy creamy crunchy bits ensure its success.

Try the Bread and Butter Pudding and a slice of Apple Pie
Or a couple of Meringues – you can diversify.
I'm flushed with nostalgic lust for baked Rice Pudding Crust.
It reminds me of school dinner – in the days when I was thinner!

Sometimes in the summer if only for a lark
The chairman draws the curtains and we all sit in the dark
Then a flaming Christmas Pudding, I near dropped my Gin & Tonic!
And the voice of Charlotte Church and the London Philharmonic.

I could go on much longer but I think you've got the gist
If you <u>don't</u> get round to joining –
Well you now know what you've missed!
Although I got here early there's some gourmets in the room
So I'll put away my pen and take up my fork and spoon.

The Girl who went Astray

Daddy thinks that I'm a model in the City's social whirl
Mummy says I'm not to tell him I've become a naughty girl.
I always was a Rebel though Daddy's little treasure
but gradually my wayward ways have drifted into pleasure.

It's not a job that all could do – I know most girls would shun it
but I would choose no other now I've been and gone and done it.
It helps to be a big girl, there's a lot of me up front –
with cars or boys, well anything, I've always gone for grunt.

I don't seek your approval of my present occupation
Don't bother me with lectures about female exploitation.
I find I have a calling – it's to help my fellow man
and they always seem so grateful – we should each do what we can.

My friend Julie does home visits in her shortie nurse's kit
Her clients seem to like it and it's for their benefit.
The Matron at the Twilight Home has said her skirts too brief
and was puzzled when she noticed red suspenders underneath.

As for Extra Special Treatments she can only guess
but notes the joy that Julie brings outside the NHS.
Her clients always pay up front – she never has to sue
and less ten percent on Wednesdays like they get at B&Q.

Some guys are quite amazing – I don't like to take their money
but who am I to change the rules between a buck and bunny.
My regulars, so generous, one says he's a Diplomat.
another's with the Income Tax – I always charge him VAT.

See my costumes in the hallway, it looks like Saddlers Wells.
My clients like variety though most choose jezebels
I do a lovely Spanish Maid and other things beside
but I don't do Traffic Warden – a girl has got her pride.

A chap called round the other day, he said his name was Peter
we caused him some embarrassment – he'd come to read the meter.
Often we have quiet times and then we have our rushes
How many on a Saturday? O, darling spare my blushes!

When I tire of doing this Social Work I'm going to write a book
on all the lovely men I've had and the jobs I undertook
I'll give it a catchy title like "Eighty Shades of Grey"
Or "How to Make a Fortune" by The Girl who went Astray.

The Office Party

Tonight's dress code is "Obvious"
It's the night of the Office Party.
Some girls will choose a classic line,
And some go loose and arty.
I think that I'll choose Ravishing
With just a shade of tarty.

I'll bait my hook in clinging red
With nothing non essential.
We've a new Trainee at six foot three –
I think he has potential.

Oh! L'Oréal you've done me proud
My hair's my crowning glory –
It might come down in the back of his car
But that's another story!

I saw him in the coffee bar
And thought he'd suit just right.
He hasn't looked my way all week
But he damn well will tonight.

This event is like the County Show –
All beef and fur and feather.
Some guys will go in Saville Row
And some in kinky leather.

They'll look around and eye us up –
Say "Have you seen her before?"
Yet it's crystal clear she's the firm's cashier
Who sits in the room next door.

He'll be putty in my hands
Once he's asked me for a dance
He'll never know what's hit him –
He hasn't got a chance.

I'll only have three hours
So I won't play hard to get
And we're all at work tomorrow
So nothing I'll regret......

    But a girl can never tell!

The Bent Brief

As a Hot Shot Legal Eagle I've been on all the courses
I spread my talents sparingly – just Criminal and Divorces.
All Matrimonial crisis are taken in my stride
Plus villainy of diverse sorts from fraud to homicide.
I find some will put their hands up – all sorrows and remorses
But to get a really good result one needs to have resources.
      Like me....

Some cases are très complique and spouses can be funny.
When love flies out the window then it all boils down to money.
"I want the divorce but all those lies and splashed across the news,
So fight the case, put on a show, but make quite sure I lose!"
A husband's fear of maintenance is logical and clear
But with my kindly guidance all his assets disappear.
      My Bill helps....

Villains are more predictable – with them I have rapport –
You get away with what you can within the Common Law.
Once the judge has been persuaded to grant Bail with Guarantor
My client has a simple choice – to stay or go offshore.
      Surprise, surprise....

For most it,s all a game once they have gone astray,
A sort of them and us with no rules about fair play.
The Police massage their evidence – such morals I can't abide
While my clerk assists the client – mouthing answers from the side.
      Carefully!

Now if you're caught red handed and you hope for some abatement
Just wait until I get to you – Don't ever make a Statement.
If the evidence is worrying and there's no better way –
Well, alibis where I come from are a hundred pounds a day.
       Plus my arrangement fee....

It offends my sense of justice to see the innocent convicted –
perhaps a rotten lawyer but more often self-inflicted.
I like fairness in the system – as a sort of referee –
I redress the balance so the Guilty can walk free.

       We don't know what the future holds – some day it might be me!

Night Panic

You must have heard that noise
It woke me with a start.
A sort of scraping scratching noise
It almost stopped my heart.

There it is again – someone's getting in.
Should I hide or should I scream, my head is in a spin?
A surge of sweat, my eyes are wide
Bursts of adrenaline.

A scratching scoring scraping sound
And then a pause – he's still around.
The silence now is frantic, alone, I feel despair.
He's nearer than ever, I just sense there's someone there.

If Fred was here I know he'd say
"There's nowt for you to fear –
It's just them trees and just the wind,
now go to sleep my dear"

But that scratching, it's not normal
there's someone in the house.
It's times like this, when panicking,
A woman <u>needs</u> a spouse.

All this scraping and the scratching – it's making me feel ill.
I'm lying here petrified – much stiller than just still
I'm <u>trying</u> to keep calm but however much I try
If that bedroom door is opened I know that I shall die.

A silence then it starts again – he's coming up the stairs
Oh God, he's going to get me – I'll start to say my prayers.
But the noise is now quite different, it vibrates against the door.
I pause and listen really hard – I've heard that noise before?

It's no longer on the landing
It's much nearer than that...
Oh no, I can't believe it –
I forgot to feed the cat!

"The Burglar"

Tonight's the night to go burgling,
It's the night of the Policeman's Ball.
If you're not doing burgling tonight,
Then don't bother to do burgling at all.

Thieving's our family profession,
It's a skill that cannot be taught.
We've lots of kin in Australia but
They're the ones who got caught.

I needn't have chosen a burglar,
My brother's a cowboy plumber.
His wife prefers him to do day work,
But the days are so long in the summer.

You won't get burgled on Tuesdays
It's the training night for us, still –
We've got to keep up with police methods,
Which we learn from watching "The Bill".

I've put dummy plates on the van,
I've loaded my Jemmy and Keys.
I've set the alarm for 1.30,
Self employed, I can start when I please.

Some secretly thank me for thieving,
They've so much that would never be missed.
To help them fill in their claim form,
I've been known to leave them a list.

So make sure you pay up on your policy,
My visit could be any day,
If you've "Neighbourhood Watch" in your window,
Perhaps tonight I'll be heading <u>your</u> way.

Nana's Advice

1. You modern girls rush in where angels fear to tread,
   We had books on etiquette which every girl had read.
   These were the golden rules – what's for the cock or for the hen,
   And if it looked precarious we'd leave it to the men.

2. IF you're tired of aerobics and you've joined the Sisterhood,
   But dishing dirt is tedious and doing you no good.
   Do what your mother did –I'll help you all I can –
   Throw caution to the wind and find yourself a man.

3. IF he talks you into hiking see he carries the rucksack,
   When you're cycling choose a tandem – put your feet up at the back.
   Such primitive pursuits – I'd avoid them if you can,
   I've always felt that muscle bulk looks better on a man.

4. IF you're in a crowded tube and there's not a seat in sight,
   Most seated men won't stand but there's just a few who might.
   So make a moaning noise – hold your stomach with your hand,
   And then you'll have a choice of seats and leave the men to stand.

5. IF your Mini hits a pothole and your tyre has gone flat,
   And a white van pulls alongside to see just what you're at.
   Try "I think I've lost my air – have you any in your van?"
   Put on a really helpless look and leave it to the man.

6. IF you chance a one night stand with a Bill or Bob or Frankie,
   Or you find you're chatted up by an Aussie or a Yankee,
   Chances are they're thinking of a little hanky panky.
   So keep your options open – tie your bus fare in your hankie.

7. IF the after office drinkie – poo is moving into "shorts",
   Then the bill when it arrives will have its share of noughts.
   You know it's on its way but you've no idea when –
   Retreat to put some make up on and leave it to the men.

8. IF you find you're in a jewellers with a suitor or a beau,
   And the balance on your credit card's unusually low try –
   "My card is in my handbag but I can't recall my pin!"
   And perhaps hitch up your skirt a bit and leave it to the men.

9. IF your mother's told you nothing as the Wedding Day gets near,
   And you're getting in a panic though you don't know what to fear.
   Remember that since Eden girls have thought the same as you,
   Close your eyes and think of England as the men know what to do.

10. IF males are born so clever and gifted "technically"
    Why can't they work the Hoover or find Cefax on TV?
    Just <u>tell</u> them how to do it and repeat it yet again,
    But let the dears keep <u>trying</u> – we owe that to the men.

11. IF city life's a jungle with females on the prowl,
    You <u>must</u> protect your treasure – it's no use crying "foul"
    Keep him busy making money – boost his ego now and then,
    And reward him from his toiling with a little cock and hen.
    Tigers in stilettos will check out your little lamb,
    So stay alert and frisky if you want to keep your man.

12. IF you're loved one hits the big time and the money starts to flow,
    And a spending spree is called for but you don't know where to go.
    Well take the tube to Bond Street – push the boat out now and then,
    Just make a serious effort – leave the earning to the men.

13. All this good advice my dear was told me by my mother –
    Little manly gems us girls pass on to one another.
    And when the Dreaded Reaper comes at three score years and ten,
    You shuffle to one side my dear and leave him to the men...

Don't Ask Me in the Morning if I Love You

I wake up first disturbed it's not my bed
I stroke your hair, my arm against your head.
You're still asleep and mostly on my side,
I whisper "I still love you" – have I lied?
I don't know if I mean it now – it's what I'm meant to say,
I think I hear "I love you too" – by then I've turned away.

Why is it always different in the morning?
Why can't feelings of the night survive the day?
Morning light creeps in where it's not welcome,
Or I would still have held you where we lay.

Now daytime thoughts come surging through my brain,
All the pressures of my working day again.
At home my clothes are neatly on my chair,
But here – that storm last night – they're everywhere.

I dress in all the clothes I think I wore,
There'll be no sign that I was ever here,
Save last night's crumpled passion on the floor,
And traces all around of faux blonde hair.

I find my keys I murmur "I must go"
It's early but I have so much to do.
My home, a shower, a coffee – I need <u>space</u>,
Last night's events they're etched upon my face.

Don't ask me in the morning if I love you – I don't know,
My feelings, day and night, they ebb and flow.
Your picture's on my desk but I don't see it,
I only see the work that needs me now.

When evening comes it's then I know I love you,
Each time we meet it's like we start anew.
Too late by then to question wrong or right, -
It's Thursday so <u>you're</u> in <u>my</u> bed tonight.

Britannia Weeps

1. Winston, thou should't be living at this hour
   England hath need of thee.
   This sceptered isle set in a silver sea
   Is just a wreck and drifting helplessly.

2. Each day we hear our creditors say
   "They'll shortly lose their Triple A –
   Like many things it's one more sign
   Of their continuing decline"

3. A Government should defend the realm and stimulate the nation
   But little men have steered us to national stagnation.
   Like children in a fairground they strove to beg and borrow
   No thought was ever given to paying back tomorrow.

4. Such a Cabinet composed of the Islington elite
   knew less of market forces than a trader in the street.
   "We can't get the books to balance after many months of trying –
   Just tell them half the story and dumb them down by lying".

5. We've lost all national pride in the Country and the Crown –
   With such a "Liberal Elite" the only way was down.
   Plus hosts of civil servants recruited through "The Guardian" –
   "Wanted – little bearded man in polyester cardigan"

6. To spy into your rubbish and treat you like a serf
   And to put you in his surveys from the moment of your birth.
   His thousand council cameras will record your every mile –
   Its "Are you now or have you ever been?"
   "Sign in black within the square" and "Do not smile".

7. Now "Made in England" doesn't sell
   "Made in Siam" sells just as well.
   "Export or Die" you used to say,
   "We sell our goods and pay our way"

8. Bless us with one more man like you
   To show the way, to start anew,
   To say "My friends it's not too late
   To fight and not capitulate."
   Like Winston – we need such a man –
   Could he be Clegg or Cameron?

A little bit on the Side

1. My colleagues in the Typing Pool they moan about their pay,
   They start off in the morning and go on throughout the day.
   It's come to be a grudge they cannot hide,
   But the problem's solved for me,
   I'm at a nightclub until three,
   I do a bit of Belly Dancing on the side.

2. As a Lady Vicar I would vote for equal pay,
   And I'll guide my flock assiduously till Resurrection Day.
   The bishop said "Be adventurous – don't feel your hands are tied"
   The ladies of my parish are very enterprising,
   And our current parish project will probably surprise him,
   Ann Summers sends the kit and it's growing bit by bit,
   We hold "Vicars Knickers Parties" on the side.

3. As a Tax Inspector I haven't any friends,
   It's boring in the evenings and worse at the weekends.
   I read this book on self improvement and at last I've turned the tide,
   Now I'm a Children's Entertainer and they scream and laugh and love me.
   It's a perfect Tax free hobby on the side.

4. If it's Amateur Theatricals they'll mention Charlie Brown,
   For many years I've been the best Producer in the town,
   Grand opera and musicals are taken in my stride.
   Most chorus girls are willing but I find there's usually one,
   Who'll be a quicker learner when the others have all gone –
   So I give <u>her</u> Extra Coaching on the side.

5. I do shift work for the Council and my time I do divide –
   I book the errant motorist and Stock Deal in the side.
   A bedtime read for me is the Economist and F.T.
   I need to check the markets every day.
   You can't run an Aston Martin on a Traffic Warden's pay
   Without some serious speculation on the side.

6. At eighteen stone and six foot three
   I knew the Police Force was for me
   But all is not as it appears I must confide.
   Not a word to C.I.D. but Debt Collecting is for me,
   I get ten per cent commission on the side.

7. As your Local District Judge I have justice on my side,
   I'm paid to know who's truthful and who's lied.
   When they see my scarlet gown and my pretty little wig
   Some villains are respectful – but most don't give a fig.
   In truth I have a quirk I cannot hide,
   When the day is done and my customers have gone
   I do Female Impersonations on the side.

8. Estate Agents and Valuers have a policy to try,
   And create a phantom shortage – it keeps the prices high.
   I sell other people's homes – No camera's ever lied?
   But a property of forty feet I'll make look eighty wide.
   Sometimes one comes along I can buy in for a song –
   They're my Little Speculations on the side.

9. The Landlord of our local is in the Good Pub Guide,
   His beer sales are massive, he's well known countrywide.
   All his drunkards when they fall
   Are lined up against his wall,
   He runs Alcoholics Anonymous on the side.

10. I'm his Barmaid – name of Shirl
    The regulars think I'm quite a girl,
    As they watch me pulling pints "London Pride".
    My fella's six foot three – that's quite enough for me,
    And I have a Sugar Daddy on the side.

My Treasure

1. Past oast houses and meadows I steer my Aston Martin,
   Most users of the highway don't know the Le Mans Mark Two.
   The polishing is finished my adventure is just starting,
   After 70 years she <u>looks</u> as she did when she was new.

2. You won't have seen too many – dark green and pretty dear,
   With straps across the bonnet and a slab tank at the rear.
   In my flying jacket and goggles I really look the part,
   A passing apparition – it could break a maiden's heart.
   When I stop at zebra crossings the brakes give out a squeal,
   Girls dream of sitting on my left with Biggles at the wheel.

3. But like so much in life – reality is cruel,
   Such silly posing is short lived as a general rule.
   Old cars are nothing like the chariots they appear –
   They're cold and unpredictable and drive you to despair.
   The cost in time is crazy and the pleasure somewhat forced –
   So most are owned by bachelors or the recently divorced.

4. Like any exotic pet you get to know it's foibles,
   In some the steering judders and in others it just woibbles (!)
   I know my tappets rattle; you can hear my gears whine,
   You get to love those noises – she's chattering all the time.

5. Swing her with the starting handle – give it a quick twist,
   And do retard the ignition or you'll get a broken wrist.
   Just one shot of the Kygas and the carbs will give a cough,
   When the pressure's up to thirty pounds it's safe to say "We're off".

6. The loud pedal's in the middle with the footbrake on the right –
   And don't ever forget – it could be worse than just a fright!
   She's set up fine for me; I won't let others have a go.
   They're sure to smash the front in - I'm firm, I just say "No".

7. As you push her through the gears you can really feel her go
   I mean to line the pedals up so I can heel and toe.
   You'll go a little faster with the windscreen folded flat,
   But flies get in your teeth if you drive around like that.

8. "Can't you slow it down a bit", you hear the passenger beg,
   As the carpets come detached and the wind blows up their leg.
   I once raced through a puddle and the water reached my knee,
   All round I've done some stupid things – That's just between you and me!

9. The final drive is groaning – is the bevel giving out?
   It's working life is ending – of that there's little doubt.
   Don't slam the door too hard – there's a problem with the lock,
   And don't fiddle with the dashboard or you'll get an electric shock.

10. We must pray it doesn't rain as the wiper motor's dodgy,
    And the brakes don't work too well with the linings wet and stodgy.
    The splines are getting worn - when I brake they make a clunk,
    But that clicking is quite normal from the S.U. petrol pump.

11. These cars weren't built for traffic queues they always overheat,
    Then half your water boils away and dribbles down the street.
    The steering's pulling to the left – was that a pot hole that I hit?
    I couldn't see too clearly as the side screens flap a bit.

12. There's a funny petrol smell – has my banjo nut gone slack?
    It's the broken piston rings that cause the smoke trail out the back.
    The ignition light is flashing – the magnito's on the blink –
    Yes, she's definitely slowing – we've broken down I think!

13. "You go home by bus – I'm staying sitting in this seat,
    Someone will pinch the lamps if I park up in the street".
    "Look at that old banger!" I hear the peasants say,
    As lonely cold and wet I wait – for the man from the AA.

"Come on, Get on with it!"

The first voice that I ever heard echoed up the birth canal
It was the midwife's coaxing me "Come on, Get on with it."
And so it's been throughout my life – that phrase that's so banal
When all I really wanted was to do the opposite.

I remember on my potty I was dreaming childish things
When mother's voice awakened me "Come on, Get on with it"
Once she'd had the baby it was time to spread her wings
And I knew once I'd been pottied someone would babysit.

They packed me off to boarding school "to speed me up a bit"
I couldn't wait for Fridays – to lie soaking in the bath
But the time so allocated was six minutes and a half
Then the beating in the door would start "Come on, Get on with it."

On one enchanted evening just us two beneath the moon
Standing by the bus stop where the street lights were not lit,
She murmured "I won't rush you but my bus is coming soon,
So *if* you're going to kiss me can you please get on with it".

Nocturnal activities are not for the faint hearted
I was slowish to get going but just fine once I got started.
The wife looked quite delightful in her pinkish negligee
Though I thought she had a headache until I heard her say
"I know what's on your mind – we don't need a plebisite
So tonight for once stop talking and just get on with it".

I got used to being a married man a state you can't surpass
Though she gave me the run around – at least it kept me fit.
"My mother's coming later – you were going to mow the grass,
Can you clear the children's toys away and please get on with it".

At Rotary on Thursdays I was in my comfort zone
Till my turn to do my job talk then I nearly had a fit.
I explained about my work and my problems in the home –
I could feel the whole room groaning "Oh, please get on with it".

But my Golden Wedding Speech I remember was a hit
Everyone was laughing – I saw no fed up signs.
Then my dear wife tugged my jacket – said "Come on get on with it"
And fifty years caught up with me and I forgot my lines.

Just last month in the Hospice I was chatting to the nurse
She explained "We have a problem – now you don't have to commit,
but we're short staffed every Friday and the weekends are much worse
So if you plan to hang your clogs up would you please get on with it".

Well now I'm up in Heaven, reading poems to my friends
They're so happy and contented no more targets to fulfil.
They don't want me to hurry – "Pen a verse that never ends, –
Go on, stretch it out a bit – We've got eternity to kill".

Dear Adelaide,

I've just received your letter – four weeks was rather long,
To reach me here in England from your home in Goolagong.
We're quite used to disruptions – another postal strike –
And my bin is overflowing – the Council now do what they like.
The land's still green and pleasant and I know you'd love the view
But in country lanes there's muggings – it's no longer what you do.

There'll always be an England whilst there's a Corner Store
That's open when you need it with "Patel" above the door
But the England of the postcard, the England of the song
England for the English – all that has nearly gone.
We're all now Europeans and call ourselves EU
And we never mention Nelson or Drake or Waterloo.
We've learned to love the Germans – who were good at starting wars
But all that's now forgotten when we queue to buy their cars.

Whatever crisis happens no one takes the blame
The hospitals are filthy and our towns are much the same.
When you left here for Oz we thought we were well off
But now too many officials have their noses in the trough.
To learn of other cultures we would fly to foreign lands
But England's cultures changing – I've seen policemen holding hands.
The church once stood for standards and cared for every waife
But things are very different now – no little boy is safe.

Villains go unpunished and crime has its reward
When burglars get counselling and victims are ignored
Most crime is drug related and the police do catch a few
But Adelaide don't panic, they'll not send them out to you!
Remember, you bought "Lady Chatterley" and let me have a look
We thought it was so naughty – well now it's a Set Book.
The television's dreadful and no one seems to care
Our standards have been slipping since the time of Tony Blair.

The population's rising now but due to immigration –
If it carries on much longer there won't be a British Nation.
When you were last in England our books were in the black
But now we're nearly bankrupt – Don't think of coming back!
If I promise not to winge and I learn some kangaroo
Can I go and pack my billabong and come and live with you?

    Your loving sister
             Ethel x

Will's " The Seven Ages"

Will, you need updating, you've done well to last this long
Four hundred years unaltered is now thought overlong.
Gilding Lilies can be tricky but some effort should be made
So I'll start with "As You Like It" and update that masquerade.

    Muling Infants are passé but puking still prevails
    And Schoolboys still do whining and creep to school like snails.
    Lovers don't do furnaces and texting's lost on you
    As must be morning after pills and TV pay to view.

    We still have swearing Soldiers but no beards in the ranks
    And cannon's mouths are obsolete – they go to war in tanks.
    The Judge with fair round belly hasn't changed that much
    But justice is dispensed with a much lighter touch.

    Your sixth age is the old guy – we call them now Retired
    They're all away on cruises – some trips are quite inspired –
    Any "slippered pantaloons" will be kept for fancy dress
    Try Warners Wrinklies Weekends at Nidd Hall or Skegness.

    And when the Final Age gets near – remember teeth and eyes
    And all those other horrors old age personifies.
    Well at that final age "sans everything"'s spot on
    Dumped in the local Council Home with all your savings gone.

    P.S. "Will, the piece you wrote is so well loved,
          so timeless and enduring.
            Perhaps we should leave it as it is" –
            "That's very reassuring!"

De Profundis

My life's run its course, no hope can I see
Black waves of depression now wash over me.
Everything's pointless; I'll make one last call
And then close my eyes and curl into a ball.

People keep asking "How are you today?"
So they know something nasty is heading my way
It's true I do moan a lot, nothing seems right
But my future's as dark as one endless night.
My dreams are all nightmares of crisis and woe –
Of panic and pain from my head to my toe.

I know some face the world not a hair out of place
And view me as pathetic – a big waste of space
But they can't see the crisis – they push when I pull
My cup is quite empty while theirs is near full.

The ring of the postman will give them a thrill
But for me it just heralds a summons or a bill.
They're moved by "Aida", it's stirring for them
But the music I choose is Verdi's "Requiem"
Those souls crying out in their last agonies
It captures my mood – I go down on my knees.

I drop in at funerals and sit at the back,
I'm hardly observed as I always wear black.
Some widow there asked if I'd pass on a note
Which she'd written out for me to put in my coat.
And she seemed quite certain that I'd see him first –
That I'd shortly be joining the souls of the cursed.

No sane man would choose to see everything black
Or welcome the thought of the next heart attack.
It's so deep in my psyche – I make this confession –
I know that my problem is Manic Depression.
Each evening I stand by this top window sill,
How long must I wait for a Happiness Pill?

Brigitte's Smile

"When I was young my legs were long
My bust was firm my arms were strong
This is my world where I belong –
St Tropez Beach in a golden thong
And to crown it all as I tripped along
— my smile.

Whenever I went off the rails –
Long boozy nights with hungry males.
When all my life was heads and tails
All frizzy ends and broken nails
I had one thing that never fails
— my smile.

Too soon I joined the mating game
I married and I changed my name.
And then at last I tasted fame –
A movie star of great acclaim.
I lost old friends and new ones came.
Of me just one thing stayed the same
— my smile.

But now I'm old, seem to have shrunk
My hair is white, my eyes have sunk
My worldly goods a trunk of junk.
My little grey cells have done a bunk –
Can't tell a mongrel from a skunk –
And all I've left when I'm not drunk's
— my smile.

Cheers, English!!"

I'll Make my Escape on the A28

I've paid all my taxes and honoured my wife
My nose to the grindstone for most of my life
Now I'm part of the scenery the last of the few
If Reggie Perrin could do it I damn well can too.

I don't know the day and I don't know the date
But you'll see – you won't have much longer to wait
Some husbands just moan and some hesitate
But a few with the bottle go on to tempt fate.

Superfluous husbands whose life is so bleak
That they dare slip their leads and escape so to speak.
This time it's for real – it's not hide and seek
"Not another one gone? That's four in a week!"

I'll jump in the car, take the A28
I'll drive to the docks and perhaps emigrate
I might need my passport – is it up to date?
If it's not I'll hide up in the boxes of freight.
First the A28, the A28, I'll make my escape on the A28.

I'll become a deck hand on a yawl or a sloop
I'll haul up the sheets and I'll live on fish soup
Or stowaway, then escape when we reach Guadeloupe.
I'll be free, I'll be me, I'll be so cock a hoop.

They'll say when I've gone "Did you hear about Freddie..?"
    Oh no! It's THE VOICE! I jump up, I'm unsteady,
    "Two hours on the sofa and still hugging your Teddy –
    Enough of daydreaming your supper is ready!"

Brown Eyes Blue

I love my little sister
I've stuck to her like glue
I've let her have my bangles
And a squirt of my shampoo.
If she has a problem
She turns to you know who
But what she's gone and done to me –
It's turned my brown eyes blue.

I met him in the Coffee Bar
I thought, I like you feller
He smiled and said his name was Jo
I told him mine was Bella.

Well he's sitting in our kitchen
Having coffee with my sister
I saw how they were holding hands
And guess that he'd just kissed her.

I don't think I can make a scene
It's put me in a stew – but
No way she wears my bangles
For their cosy rendezvous.
She didn't know I knew him
So there's nothing I can do
But when your sister bags your mister
It don't half make your brown eyes blue.

"Recycled Fools & Horses"

1. "You'll have heard of Derek Trotter, I'm an Independent Trader
   And my firm is well regarded from Peckham to Grenada.
   From Income Tax and VAT – we're champion evaders
   And now we've got the message as Recycling Crusaders.

2. Everyone's recycling – we deal in lead and copper
   And we can keep a secret if its origin's improper.
   If lead is from the Parish Church or copper from the steeple
   You don't overdo the questions when you deal with dodgy people.

3. Recycling's the current craze and we can make a nicker –
   You melt it down and roll it out and sell it to the Vicar.
   Some deals are far too good to miss unless you're off your trolley
   I sniff them out before the rest – don't want to be a Wally.

4. Our "Peckham <u>Recycling</u> Proficiency Certific<u>ate</u>"
   Proclaims to all our customers the values that we advocate
   Presented to young Rodney for not falling off his trike
   Amended and Recycled it now looks quite business like.

5. Always down The Nag's Head someone has some Kit to sell
   I pay in cash, no VAT, it helps my clientele
   Then in a flash I move it on – no invoice or recording
   One day it's in the next its out – recycling's rewarding

6. But not that hookey gear I saw stacked up in Boyce's shed –
   So hot it was still glowing – it nearly knocked me dead.
   "If the Old Bill happens to call at time inopportune
   Marlene will be back to visiting you on Sunday Afternoon"

7. We always keep stock moving - yes, you've got the right impression
   We're trying to build a nest egg before the next recession.
   If we follow the Trotter Motto, you know "He who dares..."
   Well this time next year Rodders we could both be millionaires"

"The Night Shift"

By the Light of the Silvery Moon
I walk my beat, know every street
And the folks that I meet –
Like Sid – He just opened up in June,

His Greasy Spoon will lift the gloom on the rainiest day
Look in if you're passing this way.
He's a gift for the earliest shift
They queue at his door, he opens at four – quite soon

At five's when the papers arrive, Dead on
Great bales of the Mail and the Star
Can't carry them far, he parks where he can
But no time to stop, he's off to his next drop.
Big Stan – he's our delivery man.

That's Clare, I can smell her perfume
Quite soon she'll be back in her bed
And be sleeping till noon.
Nice girl, pretty good so I've heard
Like me she's another night bird.
Her choice – perhaps I shouldn't presume.

There's Gran with her bucket and broom
She's done The Nags Head Bar & Saloon
Since I was a lad.
Poor soul, what life has she had?
Come dawn she'll stagger away
It's like that every day – so sad.

Across in the square I can just see the glow
Of the Fire Station lights – engines ready to go.
This week it's Blue Watch – at the ring of the bell
All aboard and they're off like a bat out of hell.

While here in the park curled in his cocoon
Like a pile of old rags is Paddy Mulhoon
Just sleeping it off here under the moon
You'd think he was dead like Tutankhamun.
No bother to me to let sleeping tramps lie,
My favourite tune can be his lullaby.

Our little town will soon be awake
It's the end of my shift, I sign off at daybreak
Each night of the week I'll be out here again
Policing my town in the fine or the rain
And yes, I'll be humming That Tune.

"If..."

If I had a wealthy aunt, I'd be her blue eyed boy
And she would meet the bills for all the pleasures I'd enjoy
She'd say "Pop down to Monte dear and take the Maserati
Or jet to the casinos of New York or Cincinnati"

It's not going to be easy there are skills that must be learned
To face each daily challenge yet appear so unconcerned.
If I take to being a Playboy she might buy me a yacht
And then the girls can ambush me for everything I've got.

As auntie's protégé she'd want me to go astray
To charm the pants off starlets and to live just for today
"I've left it a bit late dear for the pleasures of the flesh
Make up for what I've missed – try the souks of Marrakesh"

Each night around the roulette wheel I'd live on G & T
I'd stick to single numbers and I'd gamble until three
And then with all my winnings stuffed casually in my pocket
I'd drift up to the penthouse with my confidante or poppet.

My suits I'd buy in Paris, from a House in St Germaine
My shirts in Singapore and my shoes, of course Milan.
I'd smile on those who serve me and tip like a millionaire
And I'd not forget the postcards to my aunt in Eaton Square.

But:
I've seen a certain something in those lounge lizards and rakes
Which I think in me is lacking – I've just not got what it takes.
When I sit I try to slouch with a languid sort of air
But no one seems to notice or no one seems to care.

When I tried out my come hither look – to Playboys no great issue –
My target girl looked quite concerned and offered me a tissue.
I love brown corduroys and hairy Harris Tweed
Which I've not seen Playboys wearing –
They're a different sort of breed.

>Well in fact there is no aunt
>Who'd fund me to gallivant
>So it's likely that I shan't
>Ever be the new Hugh Grant!

>Sorry Liz....

Wrinkles Don't Hurt

When you get old you'll find changes occur
Some lose their teeth and for some it's their hair.
You'll have aches in your back and pains in your feet
And you'll hate the cold, and yet can't stand the heat.
Your voice of respect to a child's will revert
But the one saving grace is your wrinkles won't hurt.

You'll need to move house if your stairs are too steep
And the sight of an armchair could put you to sleep.
Friends from forever their names you'll forget
And bits that were dry you might find have gone wet
The doctor will give you some pills to insert
But look on the bright side – your wrinkles won't hurt.

You might know the day but you won't know the date –
Just remember meal times and your bicarbonate.
Reminisce with old friends and recall yesterdays –
Just have a good laugh and slacken your stays.
If it's fine, take a stroll with Beryl or Bert
Growing old can be fun and your wrinkles won't hurt.

The Knock on the Door

You all have a sound with which you have rapport
A sound that's so special you cannot ignore.
Perhaps the cheers in the stands when the home team score
Or the wind in the rigging when sailing offshore.
You must have a sound that you know you adore –
For me it's the thrill of a knock on the door.

For some, modern sounds are the ones they embrace –
Cars screeching away at the start of a race
Or the roar of the crowd at a steeplechase.
For others just the bustle of the market place
Or that Lancaster bomber returning to base.
For me it's the thrill, but I've told you before,
That nothing quite equals a knock on the door.

I think that was the door! – I leap from the settee
I slide down the hall, a quick turn of the key.
Hope springs eternal this time it will be
The Securicor man with a parcel for me.
A gift from my lover – sent on a whim?
And why does the dog always think it's for him?

Modern Verse

Some guy gave me a Book of Poems, I left it on the dresser,
I'm sure he thought that such a book is certain to impress her.
What happened next astounded me – it's really quite perverse,
But accounts for why this little tale is written down in verse.

Each time I thought I'd open it I spotted my "Hello",
And then I saw a picture of that Aussie Russell Crowe
Up close to some starlet on a yacht in Monaco –
I guessed that what they have in mind they won't need mistletoe.

So a "Host of Golden Daffodils" is not my cup of tea
OK for my old grannie but it doesn't click with me
Does anyone care tuppence who was Wordsworth's Confidante
Just tell me who's that Bimbo rhyming with Hugh Grant?

Remember "beaded bubbles winking at the brim"
Just perfect for my granddad – that image suited him.
But a girl now needs to know who's featuring with whom
And who's been caught in a honey trap on a Monday afternoon.

Well, I was dusting round that book of verse – I know it sounds absurd
But the book fell open on the floor and I saw a naughty word!
Who'd ever think that poetry'd catch up with modern life –
That it isn't just Pam Ayres and poems about the wife.

Now I'm hooked on reading Modern Verse – no papers for a week –
Some poems are quite outrageous and some of them quite chic.
Others are mysterious, inscrutable, oblique –
The best of them I laugh out loud and some of them I shriek.

But I still read "Hello".

A Turkish Evening

Last Friday we thought we'd stroll along
To our local Turkish Restaurant.
A place some note – just say OZ and UR
Perfect for the gastro – connoisseur.

The Menu glows with Eastern Promise
That would convert the doubting Thomas
Mezzes, sish kebab, pirzolia
Delicious wines from Anatolia.

The buffet display would make your jaw drop
Glazed lamb and musakka and escalope
Then what I saw – my eyes went pop –
Was the Couscous with an Eye on top!

The Band struck up just as we'd been told
And the Dancer appeared in her red and gold
So random and yet so controlled –
A Salome from a centrefold.

And the Eye followed her around the floor
Her every move I know it saw
With her it was having its last rapport
There were tears when it blinked though I can't be sure.

The meal progressed and the evening shone
But I was blind to such goings on.
I needed to know that the Eye was still there
That resentful eye with the glassy stare
And the Couscous with the Eye upon –
Then I looked again and it was gone!

In the kitchen I'm told there's a bowl of eyes
Each waiting its turn to blink out its goodbyes.
Checking to see just where it's heading –
To a Rotary Dinner or a Turkish Wedding
But not ever today or ever tomorrow
No Couscous Eye could I ever swallow!

"OZ" and "UR" – any slight similarity to a known Restaurant is just a coincidence.

The Country Walk ?

I've noticed as I walk along that females all seem much the same –
Indecisive – some smile at me and know my name
And others – well, I can't complain
It's just like this, let me explain.

They stop and look in windows and fiddle with their hair
If it's not their nails its make up needing some repair.
A nice walk in the country, or am I being unfair?
Why won't they walk like men do with some hope of getting there?

Waiting outside Smith's or Boots with a chap I see each week
Our patient eyes say everything there is no need to speak.
I swear mine roll right over at the sight of a new boutique
And always on a Monday when she meets her girly clique.

She knows I'm faithful and devoted
With a patience sugar coated.
Chaps like me are often voted
Quite outstanding and promoted.

If she'd just be Decisive, she said "Let's have a walkie"
But we haven't left the High Street so that's another porkie.
I might have guessed from the way she dressed
Just another "walkie talkie".

How can she chat from 2 till 4
I feel we've hardly left the door
But then, I should have said before,
I'm just the family Labrador.

"Charity Shopping"

I said "Let's go Charity shopping" – like you do
And in our little town there's quite a few.
For every ache and pain there's a charity shop the same
And to say they're full of tat is just untrue.
I know they take the blame and put other shops to shame
But I can't resist a bargain – nor can you.

Age Concern UK, I go in there every day
And I won't raise an objection to visit Cat Protection –
Some days I try the lot, well like you do.
It's known that our Sue Ryder is a very good provider
And just the place to go for nearly new.

There's the latest fashion looks and videos and books
From all around the globe – and the E.U.
You can find that trendy label and the speeches of Vince Cable
So we flock to where it's cheapest – like you do.

They're not like normal shops where one goes to purchase frocks
They don't care for stuffy folk who make a fuss.
I bought a chiffon nightie, it was huge and it was flighty –
It was crafted for a hippopotamus.
But then I was pretty certain it would make a bathroom curtain
That I hope will not be too diaphanous.

At the Oxfam shop it was just a whistle stop
I'd popped in to do a swap – well like you do.
But there was such a queue – I wanted navy blue –
That I said I'd call back later – like you do.

Then I saw the woolly jumpers – like you do
And said "Darling at these prices I'll have two"
And then I saw the tops and what with prices in the shops
I thought I'd push the boat out – like you do.

At the British Heart Foundation you get great sophistication
And a little room for fittings and a loo
There's a smarter conversation and they'll do an alteration
If you make a small Donation – like you do.

The Mermaid

A mermaid sat upon a rock acombing of her hair
When she did spy a cargo boat on the horizon there.
She took up her little mirror and she flashed a sunny beam
And straight away the little ship towards her it did steam.

A sailor boy he spotted her asitting prettily
And questioned "Did you flash that light?" she replied "Yes it was me,
I wasn't trying to lure you upon these awful rocks –
It's just that I've got serious trouble with me locks"

"When you think of mermaids, you think golden tresses
A few of us wear shells for tops but none of us wear dresses
I've used up all my L'Oreal – I'm in an awful plight
I need another bottle if poss before tonight"

"Young lady I can see from here your hair is in a mess
And I will waste no time, your problem to address.
I've been around the cargo hold – we've got a crate or two
And with the captain's leave we'll start throwing some to you.

Most they split upon the rocks and ran into the sea
And she was shouting "Harder, throw the ruddy things at me"
Lots and lots of L'Oreal was spilling on the sand
But they just kept on throwing till one landed in her hand.

"You're all so very kind", the sailors heard her cry
"Sorry I didn't swim to you I'd only just got dry"
She couldn't thank them all enough the favour to repay
But said "I'll look real beautiful when you come back this way"

By the time the sailors left there were bubbles down the coast
But in the mermaids cave the bubbles were the most.
All the mermaid's now have really shiny mops
And they say that's how the little waves got their frothy tops!

"Shared Space"

Avoid the town of Ashford where the "Shared Space" draws you in
Where pedestrians play chicken with the car
If you're fit and active the scheme may be attractive
But most of you will not get very far.

They've dug up all the kerbs and removed the traffic lights
If you find a little corner you should wait
You could be there till evening but at least you'll be breathing
Here those not in a car are second rate.

We used to wait along the pavement until the bus arrives
Now we huddle in a bit of no man's land
That was how it's planned and we don't know where to stand.
This crazy scheme plays games with people's lives.

So keep well clear of Ashford, don't ever go to shop
There are fairer games of chance or tempting fate.
The odds are stacked against you – you'll be in a sorry state
If you think "This time the car is going to stop."

There is Still Time....

Yesterday all my troubles seemed so far away
Or have I lost a day – the games that memories play.
Of my troubles long ago – don't ask me, you've no need to know –
Save men can't reap unless they sow.

For far too long I played the game,
The firm came first, I took the strain.
My life a Punch and Judy show of money, deals and vertigo –
Then I switched off the dynamo.

I removed my plate from the office door
Took my final trip down the corridor
They begged me to stay, I didn't reply
I'm the one who escaped from their River Kwai.
The book is shut now but in truth to tell
I would never go back – not a hope in hell.

I sent them the keys, they collected the car
And my bonus I spent with Eurostar.
A Rolling Stone? – Well my response
"Will it dawn on you that you only live once?"

If your life is in commerce or arts and crafts
Don't leave it too long or you'll die in the shafts.
There's no need to wait for the first heart attack
Just grab what you've left and never look back.
This bum with the beard and the old guitar
He escaped from the treadmill to Shrangri-la.

"I bought the bloody pie from Tesco's"

"Oh yes your worship, no your worship
Very much obliged your worship".
"Send her up to Level Two –
A jury will know what to do".

"Straight out the box and in the cooker"
A likely tale! I say we book her.
"She mixed it in his apple pie"
The officer will testify.

A very nasty case your Honour
Killed her man with belladonna.
Though not a trace of any on her
The papers say that she's a gonna.

With poisons you can smell the guilt
And now she's in it to the hilt
"Bought it from the Tesco shop –
Well where's the proof? – She'll get the drop".

A rotten brief – her chances plummet.
No one believes she never done it.
The judge proclaims in a sombre voice
"On what I've heard I have no choice".

You never know what's in a pie
You get it wrong and you can die
She killed her man – there's no excuse
And round her neck they placed the noose.

The general view up here in Heaven's
"The Jury's wrong about one in seven"
So if you buy your man a sweet
Take care – Hang on to the receipt.

A Family Fortune

The ancestors look down from guilded frames
They each give me a disapproving stare
And looking up I see their haughty faces
All scandalised that I'm their rightful heir.

The title should have passed to father's brother
But fate decided that was not to be.
Uncle Freddie blew a fuse when he was plastered
And the Roulette of Succession stopped with me.

Perhaps they didn't like their portraits painted
Or when completed knew they'd have to pay
The artists, could they all have smelled of garlic
Had a po-faced string of gentry to portray.

Should I lift them down and place them round the skirting
At least the most pretentious eight or ten
And let them have a taste of being humble
As the cleaners and the staff gaze down on them?

I said "Look – unless you try to change your habits
you'll finish in the attic pigeonholed
to join the ranks of former generations
and like them to glower at spiders in the cold."

For weeks and weeks we've trawled around the galleries
It takes much longer when you're newly rich
The West End is now depleted, our buying spree completed,
You chose then flash the Visa or the Switch.

The vans have just delivered all our treasures
It'll take some time to place them round the Hall
We can shuffle them or move them if we need to
Let's start and get a few hung on the wall.

In the Drawing room I think we'll have the Renoir
His olive trees remind me of Provence
Yes on the north wall there in place of grandpa
A lot of our new treasures come from France.

Monet's "Waterlillies" in the Parlour -
Christie's said he painted quite a few
Don't mix him up with Manet on the landing
Or Tracey Emin hanging in the loo.

The large Jack Vettriano will look great by the piano
And the Pool of Swimming Carp there by the harp
Just the bust of Katherine Jenkins and the Music Room is done –
She cost a bomb but aren't we having fun?

I've chosen racy ladies for my Study
Some Spanish nudes by William Russell Flint
His water colours to me are near perfection
Steamy and risqué?   Well just a hint.

Around the Entrance hall we'll have Picasso's
If not by him then by his next of kin
Together they will make a jolly statement –
as the man said "Can't say which are genuine?"

You'll have heard I also won the Euro millions
Such fortune finds its way to very few
I cannot think of any more deserving –
Unless of course the prize had gone to you!

(Sorry about the piarno!)

Tomorrow

I'm starting my diet tomorrow
I've purchased my last chocolate whirl
The decision is taken and unless I'm mistaken
There'll be no more of "She's A Big Girl!"
I blame all my weight on my mother –
So kind and such a good cook
"I've just spent three hours in the kitchen
Now it's your turn to eat it all up".

My wardrobe just smells of elastic
Every garment is baggy and full
All the outlines are sketchy and everything's stretchy –
My tents of polyester and wool.
Most dresses just hang from my shoulders
Like Britannia dressed in a sack
I try not to look too conspicuous
And pray beige will make a comeback.

So:-
I've been round the house with a basket
And gathered up temptations galore
They're spread out all over the table –
When they're finished I'll not buy any more.
Tonight's my last night for a beano
With my coke and my chocolate and fudge
I'll stretch myself out on the sofa –
Soon I'll not be able to budge...

The Beginner

So you're joining our Art Class, how nice
And you've tried art before once or twice?
Yes it's quite clear that you've got great scope to improve
So I'll give you some friendly advice.

When teacher says "What can you do –
show me a picture or two"
Don't pull up your vest and show her your chest
With that overweight dragon tattoo.

If sometimes the model is nude
You can't have her think you're a prude
Take a grip on your pencil or other utensil –
You'll find you soon get in the mood.

You'll shortly improve by degrees
Have no problem with woodland and trees
But faces take years and can drive you to tears
You <u>might</u> find you've <u>no</u> expertise.

But give it a try for a term
They'll give you some weeks to confirm
Your skills should explode once you've been showed
By Joanne of The Fibreglass Sperm.

What the hell when you start on the course
If you can't draw a cow or a horse
A few weeks with our team and you'll find it's a scream
But our humour is arty – not coarse.

The Prodigal Husband

Dear John,

I'm sorry that they sacked you and so soon after we parted –
Your lawyers should have thought of that and not been so soft hearted
Those years we were together when I cared for you so much
Have put me in your Pension Plan so I'll always keep in touch.
You drove out of my life without an au revoir
Some day I <u>might</u> forgive you but you're not getting the car.

You always seemed exhausted when you came home at night
Every time the phone rang I'd see you get up tight
Then I'd make you cocoa and soothe your fevered brow
How could I be so stupid – I can't believe it now!
Lord knows where you went to pursuing your affair –
While I slaved in the garden you were planting seeds elsewhere.

Why are men so stupid – can't they value what they've got?
You'd struggle in a rowing boat and think you're Captain Scott
I could have told you years ago you're not an Errol Flynn
And now that it's unravelled can't you see the mess you're in?
You had no cause to wander off you really had the best
Well there you are I've said my bit and got it off my chest

Your bouquet has now arrived – it makes a lovely sight –
It reminds me why I loved you – why I missed you every night
But the pain of your departure has left a dreadful scar –
And remember after all these years I know your repertoire.
The children need the two of us but I'm told the law forbids
That if <u>ever</u> I forgive you I still keep the kids.

You're little poem was magic John and it will help your cause
But after such an awful year I feel I need a pause.
I've booked to fly to Florida so can you feed the cat?
The key is where it always was – underneath the mat.
And <u>if I</u> do forgive you then I'll still keep the house
To remind you of the grief you caused

                              Your ever loving spouse
                                        Jane x

PS.
The garden needs attending to as well!

Maggie May   (too late for Dolly Parton)

I beg you Maggie May don't steal my man
with your glamour and your style I know you can
Bill is weak and you are strong
you'd tire of him before too long
Oh Maggie May I beg don't steal my man.

At school before you went away you always were so pretty
and now you've added glamour after two years in the city
You've cast a spell across the village
please don't use it now to pillage
and mess up all the plans I've made for Bill.

Don't turn his head it isn't fair
us two we've not been anywhere.
My scheme for Bill's – to be his wife
and stay on here for all our life.
Just tell me you've no plans to steal my man.

He needs my love, he's not your toy
He's just a lovely country boy
So while you're here just pick another
Pick anyone, check out his brother,
Just Hands Off, Maggie leave my man alone.

" TWGGS"

(Tunbridge Wells Girls Grammar School)

Five little Twiggs Girls as a general rule,
Meet up every morning to walk along to school.
All feel pretty jolly – its half past eight,
We must be going now – we don't want to be late.

Five little Twiggs Girls keen to do their best,
Remember the date today – it's the history test.
But one's forgotten her homework – she's rushed back to her door,
The other girls kept walking on so now there were four.

Four little Twiggs Girls each with a happy smile,
Will they stay together? Well only for a while.
One spotted Arthur, who she said she had to see,
She ran off to meet him and then there were three.

Three little Twiggs girls – school isn't very far,
One popped into a sweet shop to buy a chocolate bar.
The others hoped they'd get a piece but time was ticking by,
So those two kept on walking – I'm sure you know why.

Two little Twiggs Girls nearly at the school,
Heard music from a mobile – sounded really cool.
Then one heard her mother say "Your school bag's on your bed –
If it wasn't fastened on my girl you'd forget your head!"

So that one fled the other way aiming for her home,
And the other little Twiggs Girl carried on alone.
Just one little Twiggs Girl who was never ever late –
The school bell started ringing as she strolled through the gate.

The Vicar said ....

Learn the Ten Commandments son, or you could go astray
Keep on the straight and narrow or you'll have the Devil to Pay
So now he's taught me lots of things I didn't know before –
got me thinking of Temptations that perhaps I should explore.

I'd never thought to covet my neighbour's wife or cow
but all this Negative Guidance has got me wondering now.
You cannot seek forgiveness ness you've been dissolute –
Those Biblical Temptations hang like forbidden fruit.

And only Ten it makes you think – that cannot be the lot
there must be loads of other laws that Moses just forgot.
By then he was an old man and stone slabs can be weighty
I reckon he dropped quite a few – perhaps started off with eighty.

Course they were meant for Israelites and most are now outdated
and don't apply to boys like me - I'm unadulterated.
Like no working on the Sabbath, avoid pork of all descriptions
and never use obscenities – except about Egyptians.

When relatives come visiting don't water down the wine
and never park your chariot on a double yellow line
Hands off thy brother's concubine? –
These laws were made for Palestine.

All that "begetting" in The Bible it's like "Fifty Shades of Grey"
I'm safer with my "Motor Sport" and keeping out the way
so I think I'll miss next Sunday when the Vicars doing LUST
It'll just give me ideas where before I've not been fussed.
In his pulpit every Sunday s'pose he's got to pay his way
but it can't be right for Vicars leading lads like me astray.

Calais

We loaded up our rucksacks and we got as far as Kent
when there displayed in front of us was this advertisement
"Folkestone for the incontinent – Dover for the Continent"
So we said "Let's take the ferry" and off to France we went.

We didn't have a phrase book but we thought we'd muddle through
We knew that beds were zimmer and toiletten for the loo
I'd heard the Frogs speak English when our backs are turned
been doing it for donkeys years since Joan of Arc was burned.

The crossing was quite choppy – the sausages flew from my plate
lots of crashing and banging and the boat pulled in quite late.
Found a little bed and breakfast by the harbour wall
Madam wanted euros but we'd none of those at all.

She said "Rooms charged by the hour and it's extra for a shower"
what a tip and what a sight but what the hell just for one night.

At the corner by the jetty were they park the ships
I'd seen a froggy cafe selling Moules and Chips
where we enjoyed a plate full and some jolly comradeship
then we went back to our doss-house for well earned kip.

The couple in the room next door were having quite a brawl
expected any minute they'd come crashing through the wall
you could have got a reading on a poly-seismograph
but eventually a deal was done as both started to laugh.

I crashed out on the bed – you could feel it was still warm
and will we both be bitten to death by dawn?
Then more secrets but in French came from the double bed
And the row next door restarted as I laid my head.

We woke up early and we had a good scratch
then we went down stairs for a slanging match.
Madam had seen those bites before
but she turned quite aggressive and showed us to the door.

The altercating couple went their separate ways
and we wandered into town like a pair of castaways
It started to rain and the place was pretty dead
so we said "Let's give Folkestone a try instead?"
You can keep your Calais and your St. Tropez
so we took the ferry back to the Old U.K.

The Old Millionaire

The Old Millionaire with his elegant car
has no one to love him except his cigar
If he just had one friend they could fly anywhere
He can buy what he likes but there's no one to share.

He stands by his window shaking his head
touched only his coffee from breakfast in bed.
A past but no future to welcome the day
The rest of his life is just leaking away.

In his vast double bed one pillow stays cold
if things could be different he'd pay it in gold.
His single obsession the rule of his life
that the girl he had chosen could not be his wife.

Each morning he kisses her old photograph
then he showers and dresses and details the staff.
A life of hard work and now this dividend –
That he's made far too much – more than he'll ever spend.

Some day he will die and leave all by his Will
to that beautiful girl from The Old Vaudeville
He'd sent her red roses at the start of his life
but she said "I am married and cannot be your wife."
That girl of his dreams whom he can never own.
He's loved her forever and so he lives alone.

Dear Miss Ho

I'm leaving you this note to say
I'm going home I leave today.
I'd always dreamt of going East
to the land of Zen and the Buddhist Priest.
The choice to go and have a look
or stay at home and buy the book.

You've shown me the most amazing sights
Explained a thousand feudal rights.
The ancient Warriors and The Wall
and every type of market stall.

I've seen a hundred Temple Bells
I ate the rice and smelt the smells
but near a month of funny tums
each followed by the skids and runs.
Tried half the food of chinks and nips
and never once a plate of chips.

Seen peasants living hand to mouth
where every building must face south.
Sights I'll remember till I die
but time has come to say Goodbye.

Most find the East inscrutable,
unchangeable, immutable,
Exotic? Irrefutable
It's just for me unsuitable.

My patient Guide, you never complain
Don't chide yourself as I'm to blame
When I'm at home I'm much the same
Good Luck, sweet dreams and Thanks again
- Sorry I've been such a pain.

Salade Niçoise (or Louis stole my salad)

In the Kingdom of Sardinia was the ancient town of Nice
And the Austrians were beating at the door.
The French said "We can help you drive them back across the Alps
But Nice must then be French for evermore."

The locals knew the secret of a dish they had perfected
Would be stolen by the French – well that's what they suspected.
Two hundred years of blending to the music of guitars
And the treasure they'd created was their famed "Salade Niçoise"

The deed was done and dusted (it was 1861)
The French brought up their cannon and the Austrians were gone.
In all of military history there's few battles more absurd
Than the one to steal that secret by Napoleon the Third.

So it was by force of arms that their treasure he did clench
And the pride of the Italians was stolen by the French.
You'll have noticed it's now listed with other French cuisine
So you'd think it is a French dish – as the locals had foreseen.

Next time you go to Nice choose a cafe in the square
If you let me have some dates I'll meet you there.
We'll share a Salade Niçoise, drink a toast in Chardonnay
"To the Queen of Italian salads on which we've dined today!"

The Wine Tasting

"We're having a "Degustation" if you'd like to pop along –
A chance to meet the neighbours in Molyneux Park Road"
Though he'd seen me walk the dog his assumption was quite wrong.
I've a bedsit by the station, a humble little abode.

There's just the dog and me and we live on take-aways
Save Gino's on a Tuesday for spaghetti bolognaise –
Pity he said Friday – that's my night for Vindaloo.
Too much can blow your brains out but I'll see what I can do.

I was politely late as I'd downed some beers at home
And in deference to my new friend, I lashed out on Cote du Rhone
My usual party gift is a pack of Becks or Fosters
But create a good impression – I'll not quibble what it cost us.

Some chap in a green apron put a wine glass in my hand
A gesture well intentioned but not the size that I had planned.
I handed him my gift which I thought was etiquette
And guessed I'd find the beer if I could find the kitchenette.

My host was circulating and had put out bread and cheese
Though he must have thought his neighbours were pretty hard to please
Not a beer in sight but wine was all around.
I said "Your cheese is lovely" – he just looked at me and frowned.

His friends all seemed standoffish and they weren't too keen on wine
I thought "If they're so fussy why didn't they decline?"
I think he was having some work done –
There were boxes of sawdust about
A fact that was very fortuitous with so many spitting wine out.

Wholesale expectoration – he'd be blind not to have seen.
It really was disgusting – worse than our works canteen.
Nobody did any singing or cracked any jokes that I heard
They just nodded at each other and gurgled –
From most there was hardly a word.

Some guest then did a mumble but I couldn't really follow
As his mouth was full of wine which he didn't want to swallow.
Something to do with a Margot and a Julian locked in a cellar
He didn't say what they got up to or even if harm then befell her.
I've been to better funerals with a decent choice of beer,
Where the guests can have a knees up in a jolly atmosphere.

So –

I admit I got stuck into drinking there was nothing much else to do
And with all those half empty bottles and not even a top to unscrew.
Then the room started moving round slowly, I decided I needed fresh air
I'd had more than enough of his party and was feeling a bit worse for wear.

You'll find that at upper class functions some customs are really quite funny –
By the door was the chap with the apron and he held out a tray full of money.
His gesture it's true did surprise me, I smiled warmly and took a few notes
After all it was quite a nice ending and I headed to check on the coats.

I had no trouble finding my jacket with "Wimpy" displayed on the back
But it didn't seem to have any armholes – if it did I was losing the knack.
I fell down the steps upon leaving – there seemed more than when I arrived
But thanks to my plastic wine bottle it will please you to know I survived.

I'd thought "Oh my bottle's not needed" it was still on the shelf in the hall.
We all need some help when we're tiddly and Cote du Rhone cushioned my fall.
I'm afraid all the rest is confusion, at the limit of my recollections.
I think I gave a little wave and set off in all directions.

The Great War 1914-18   (for Annabel)

I remember my son Arthur playing soldiers with his friend
Sometimes they were English or Germans – they'd pretend
Shooting in the grass or from behind a tree
And when the game was over I'd call them in for tea.

I remember the day the Sergeant called "Your Country Needs You, son
All men are being recruited to go and fight the Hun"
His letters home were shocking – of guns and dying men –
And I thought from the onset, "Will I see my son again?"

I remember the Postman calling – the envelope bore a Crown –
Like others in their thousands to all the streets in town
It just said "Your son is missing", the news all mothers dread
"We'll tell you if we find him", but I knew my son was dead.

The Diamond Jubilee   (6th June 2012)

It's the day of the Diamond Jubilee
A day for rejoicing by Royal Decree
The Mayor and the Council will plant a tree
Then all of the Town will be making whoopee.

Poets are striving across the UK
With Editors shouting "Now no more delay,
You've had sixty years to prepare for this day!"
Is everything ready? We hope and we pray.

Some will fly flags and some will ring bells
And some will pin medals to ancient lapels.
The rich will drink toasts in the smartest hotels
But for memories and fun a Street Party excels.

We all must give thanks to the heroes who make
The thousands of pies and the jelly and cake.
Some will get drunk, some glasses will break
It's a Jubilee Party for heaven's sake!

We saw our Queen in black and white in 1953
Just a flickering image on our first T.V.
From years of war it lifted us, our pride returned that day
From the Abbey Church in London to countries far away.

Our Queen has welcomed Presidents, Ambassadors and Popes,
Launched our ships and submarines and checked the periscopes.
Every week of every year we wonder how she copes –
But sixty years in any job you get to know the ropes.

Each week you've given advice Ma'am without giving offence,
To all of your Prime Ministers (some short on common sense...)
You've outlived so many tyrants from Moscow to Beijing
And long forgotten despots whether President or King.

Your smile has held together our Diplomatic Links
Invited to the Palace for caviar and drinks,
Yet knowing that back home their freedom record stinks
You've concealed your Royal Contempt like the smile upon the Sphinx.

We pray your Reign continues to be long and trouble free.
It's only to your Majesty that we will bend the knee.
The Guardian of the Nation, The Mother of the Free
Three cheers for Her Majesty on this Her Jubilee.

Soon bells and flags and partying will sweep across the Nation,
Sixty years our Sovereign is a cause for celebration.
We'll have the best street party this town has ever seen,
And we'll join with half the world in singing "God Save the Queen".

The Gurkha Soldier

We joined the British Raj at the time of Waterloo
And for near two centuries now the Brigade's been loyal and true.
We've supported you in battles to many a glorious end –
"Never had a Country a more faithful friend" *

My grandpa, one of thousands of hardy Nepalese,
Enlisted in the army to fight the Japanese.
Cowardly dogs bark loudest – but from those Japs not a sneeze
In silent jungle warfare they had such expertise.

I lost grandpa and two uncles, many a relative and friend,
The fighting was so violent you cannot comprehend.
The Brigade lost seven thousand – that was their Peace Dividend
But through such heavy losses they saw Victory in the end.

I was with 2 Para at the Battle of Goose Green,
The Bravest of the Brave we made a fearful team –
Those lads from Argentina faced a Military Machine –
See the moonlight on fixed bayonets and how our Kukris gleam!

The Argi's not a fighting man but by God can he pray
But the Gods support the bravest in battle so they say –
So quickly on his knees and so quick for mercy begs
He dropped his gun, threw up his arms as pee ran down his legs.

We do not hate those whom we fight
With gun and knife and dynamite –
Enough that they surrender or are put to flight –
Your enemy of yesterday could be your friend tonight.

The British Brigade of Gurkhas is our chosen way of life –
To be there at your shoulder wherever there is strife.
Our calling is as fighting men – not displays in the Albert Hall
For as long as Britain needs us there'll be Tigers in Nepal.

*The Wording from the Gurkha Memorial unveiled by H.M. The Queen on 3rd December 1997.

Unnatural Selection

When I saw your name was Leslie I thought you were a bloke,
Another Leslie something from a place like Basingstoke.
And in full battle dress – no way that I could guess –
You were just another applicant to join the S.A.S.

As the Sergeant Instructor I'm not paid to have self doubt,
I knew that in a week or so I'd safely weed you out.
The tests we set are tough and we don't take second best
All physical and mental skills are carefully assessed.

That week of Self Survival in the forests of North Wales
Was to help us sort out men from boys and not from, well, females.
<u>You</u> made the place your home, yet for most it was disaster,
And you kept your team together – no one skinned a rabbit faster.

Your swimming was amazing – as if you had webbed feet.
In every test we've put you through we've rated you "elite".
I've done this job for years and I've seen some useful guys –
You're up there with the best of them – and easier on the eyes!

Down at the Firing Range you had a natural skill
And a steadiness of nerve if it came to shoot to kill.
At the end of the Mock Battle all the others were crashed out
And <u>who</u> taught you to twist the gun to get the bayonet out?

We've added up the scores, you came top in all the tests
And from a hundred applicants you clearly were the best.
You'd be a credit to the Regiment – I <u>could</u> see you as Colonel.
You're a lovely looking lass – but the problems are external.
We take tall men and short men and commoners and earls.
I should have told you sooner – it's just we don't take girls!

The Hills of Kandahar

"Put me down for Bomb Disposal Sarg" the girls will think it's cool.
You need to be born lucky – I was born in Hartlepool.
Civi Street was getting stodgy now this army job is dodgy –
But for every bomb there is a special tool.
You usually lay down flat and with your scraper start to scrat
Then up she comes like digging up a jewel.

Most army jobs are killing but mine is saving lives –
To help a few more squaddies to go home to their wives.
"Invade!" some politician said and nine years on four hundred dead.
The Army won't say why they died – just that the politician lied,
That's nine years in Afghanistan still rooting out the Taliban.

He's a fearless fighting man is your Afghan Taliban,
He answers to his God and the Koran.
Just like a peasant farmer he wears no body armour
 And he's lead by Mullah Omah and his clan.
Their crude intimidation ensures collaboration
In this timeless endless mess – Afghanistan.

We're in this arid place to protect the human race –
Buy a poppy from a hero, who got shrapnel in his face.
He was clearing a way through the furrows in the clay
When some hidden mine exploded in the dirt.
The hills of Kandahar were the last thing that he saw
Then his sight was blotted out for evermore.

Our Bomb Disposal Sarg is out there at first light
Checking out the lanes around the base.
The bravest of the brave he's got medals from Iraq,
A caring man – you see it in his face.
We know that he has guts and not just the Desert Star
And some day we know we'll see them in a hole in Kandahar.

If my luck runs out tomorrow and I'm blasted off the ground
And bits of me are lying in the desert all around.
They'll say "Son, you've earned this medal,
What you've done was marvellous –
Now go back to your mother, you can do no more for us".
I'd rather have my legs than get medals every day,
And who do you leave your medals to when your tackle's blown away?

Each night the drones go over towards the hills of Kandahar,
If they're lucky killing dozens as in an abattoir.
If it carries on for years till there's bodies wall to wall,
There's twenty million Afghans – we cannot kill them all.
Nine years is long enough – there must shortly come a day
When we fold our tents like Arabs and quietly slip away.

Lord Nelson's Lament

1. My column in Trafalgar Square is fifty metres high,
   Children ask their father "Who's that hero in the sky?"
   But heroes must be perfect men and faithful to their wife,
   The Godlike figure that you see was not me in real life.

2. I went to sea at twelve years old like many a lad before me,
   My life was moulded by the waves – turbulent and stormy.
   I learned to read the weather and the minds of men,
   For excitement and adventure I'd choose that life again.

3. Great were our successes on many a foreign sea,
   I led from the front and my men were loyal to me.
   When the fleet goes into battle you know every man's your brother,
   Loyalty is vital – we all sink or swim together.

4. Now I <u>must</u> tell you of Emma, a British Consul's wife,
   The most beautiful woman I'd beheld in all my life.
   I rescued her in Naples as the French besieged the town,
   And our hearts became entwined – I could never put her down.

5. We made our home in Merton where we entertained in style,
   Nobility vied to dine with Lord Nelson of the Nile.
   The Prince of Wales and Viscounts and Ambassadors from abroad,
   Enjoyed our hospitality – the price we could ill afford!

6. Emma was the toast of London in a certain social group,
   A model and an actress though not of a touring troupe.
   She'd sat for portraits thirty times – by George Romney no less,
   Then little Horatia came along to complete our happiness.

7. The French had executed Louis and Napoleon held the reign,
   And he'd reached a vile agreement with Charles the Fourth of Spain.
   Three hundred thousand Frenchman were massing to invade,
   England had no army which could hold back such a raid,
   But she did have press-ganged sailors from every shire and dive,
   And Pitt called us to action in eighteen hundred and five.

8. We sighted the Franco Spanish fleet just south west of Spain,
   All line astern near five miles long – we might not get that again.
   I had the bands play "Rule Britannia" and the flags say "Close engage",
   And seventeen thousand Englishmen prepared to earn their wage.

9. Hardy steered the "Victory" beneath that wintry sky,
   Into enemy broadsides – though they always fire too high.
   Then when we got alongside our thirty pounders did us proud,
   Aiming low and accurate, so fearful and so loud.

10. Fourteen men to every gun kept firing till the job was done,
    Holed up on a splintering gun deck slaves to the voracious gun.
    For four hours long they did it's bidding –
    That's how naval battles were won.

11. The French fleet we did soundly whip – with not the loss of a single ship,
    The odds were long, my lads were strong,
    From the start <u>they</u> never lost their grip.
    But a sniper got <u>me</u> in the shoulder,
    I should have heeded Hardy's call,
    "A chest of medals makes a target",
    <u>My</u> pride went before my fall".

12. Four thousand men died with me on that October day,
    Each man doing his duty – it's the price some had to pay.
    Five hundred came from England, the rest from France and Spain,
    All died for King and Country – once you're dead you're all the same.

13. News reached Plymouth to great elation,
    And bells rang out across the nation.
    "The fleet have given us a blessed day,
    We owe them a debt we can never repay".
    Yet more to my Immortal Glory,
    But one month on – another story.

14. The British tar learned long ago, "Do not expect too much"
    By bravery and training we can beat the French and Dutch.
    Through grapeshot and through cannon we will fight until we win,
    But we'll never beat the Admiralty – the enemy within.

15. Their Lordships had no further use for fifteen thousand men –
    Not ever in their lifetime would the French try that again.
    "We cannot let them off the boats – that scum might start a riot –
    The last thing Pitt's government needs is another Thomas Wyatt.
    Keep them in their battered hulks and best below the hatches,
    Then pay them off like freeing slaves – slowly and in batches".

16. If Bonaparte had landed, the consequence – you've guessed it,
    A guillotine on Tower Hill – the King's head in a basket.
    Their Lordships too had much to lose their thanks should be the most,
    But they forgot my bonny lads boxed up all round the coast.

17. There they were held for eighteen months,
    Many dying from their wounds.
    No state could treat its heroes worse,
    Such cruelty knew no bounds.
    Their Lordships knew how hard we'd fought,
    To save them from invaders,
    Now these men from their graves cry out
    "England you betrayed us".

18. Their Lordships at the Admiralty they all survived that day,
    The blood and gore of battle was a thousand miles away.
    They gave each other medals – of my men there was no thought –
    Planned my funeral procession as they sipped their vintage port.

19. Great State plans were put in place,
    To display the invincible British Race,
    A huge expense in time of war – devoid of any sanity,
    Save to elevate the Government and gratify their vanity.

20. All nations need their heroes – I was an obvious choice.
    All sing of England's Glory united in one voice,
    But your hero must be sanitised – all's fair in love and war?
    No mention must be made that your hero kept a whore.
    So my dear Emma and my daughter – they had no part to play,
    Hypocrisy by turkey cocks – it was a shameful day.

21. My Reverend brother William, a mean and stupid man,
    Was dusted down and readied as the ceremony began.
    The King gave him a peerage – though he'd never held a sword,
    And a pension for life – an undeserved reward.
    And then a hundred thousand pounds of my poor sailor's pay –
    Not a crumb of the new Earl's pudding ever came my daughter's way.

22. The two that I held dearest – who to me so much had meant,
    Were to the Government and their Lordships just a slight embarrassment.
    "That woman wears no spouse's ring – she has no claim upon our King,
    And living openly together, so brazen (is it worse?),
    We won't pay her a penny from The Navy Privy Purse".

23. My soul mate for my last five years was left to grieve in penury,
    Imprisoned in The Debtors Prison – lost all she had – her liberty.
    Hardy and my true navy friends then bailed her out and made amends,
    Told her she should flee to France or face re-arrest – there was that chance.

24. Secretly they fled to Calais where my late enemies' people dwelt.
    While in St. Paul's my tomb rose up round which an adoring public knelt.
    Horatia was fourteen then, though older than her years,
    I weep that all I left her was the name she bears.

25. Often at our family home she'd sat with the Prince of Wales,
    Amused by Admirals and Captains – regaled by navy tales.
    Now lodging with her sickly mother whose only refuge was in drink,
    Nursed her alone until she died – What did those Calais people think?

26. She pawned my medals to a Frenchman just to see the rent was paid.
    Emma died so poor and lonely and in a Calais grave was laid.
    The daughter of your National Hero an orphan in a foreign land,
    Abandoned by her King and Country – no father there to hold her hand.
    From my tears at night I could near drown,
    "Oh England how you let me down"!

27. When you drink to my Immortal Memory on each Trafalgar Day,
    Pardon that I stay seated and I turn my head away.
    Toast the sailor lads who saved you and the good ship "Victory"
    Not flawed Horatio Nelson and their Lords of the Admiralty.

In 1822 Horatia married the Reverend Phillip Ward, Vicar of Tenterden where she lived "in reduced circumstances" for the next twenty eight years. They had nine children.

It was to be 45 years after Trafalgar before Horatia at last received Royal Recognition – when Queen Victoria directed that she should be paid an annual sum for life £500.

I suspect that Lord Nelson would have been flattered but not too surprised to know that one of Horatia's great grandsons attained the highest rank in the armed services (Marshal of the Royal Air Force. Sir William Dickson, DSO, KBE etc 1905 – 1987)

"Goodbye My Love"

Sweet morphine take me in your arms your swirling mists to calm me
To float in your narcotic clouds where nothing more can harm me.
Your little pump deep in my arm is now my newest friend
Who'll gently help me on my way until I reach the end.

Soft clouds drift by above my head but I must lie reclining
You'll never know how beautiful each with a silver lining.
I sense you as you hold my hand and squeeze it ever tighter
It's not like me to drift away I always was a fighter.

Quite soon I know that I'll be gone beyond the reach of pain
Another world awaits me – you must be my Flame.
For 40 years we were a team, I wouldn't change a thing,
But hadn't planned to leave you now – Death this is thy sting.

I thank you all who loved me, who held my hand through life
I leave behind a lonely man – so proud to be his wife.
To those of you who may read this, I'm pleased I was your friend
And especially you my lover who was with me to the end.
I feel tonight my time will come before the morning dew
I wish you many happy years and I will wait for you.